SRI RAMAKRISHNA UPANISHAD

D1571542

BY

C. RAJAGOPALACHARI

Sri Ramakrishna Math

MYLAPORE MADRAS 600 004

Published by
Adhyaksha
Sri Ramakrishna Math
Mylapore, Chennai-4

**Total number of copies
printed before: 43,500**

XIV-2M 3C-12-2013
ISBN 81-7120-038-9

Printed in India at
Sri Ramakrishna Math Printing Press
Mylapore, Chennai-4

PUBLISHER'S NOTE

We have much pleasure in placing before our readers the English translation of the *Ramakrishna Upanishadam* written in Tamil by Sri C. Rajagopalachari and published by us in November, 1950.

Within this short period of three years the book has been translated into Hindi, Gūjerati, Bengali and Kannada and this undoubtedly proves the popularity of the book.

Several writers have dealt in various ways with the life and teachings of Sri Ramakrishna, the prophet of harmony of religions. But Rajaji has a unique method of presentation. Here he has retold the tales and parables of Sri Ramakrishna in such an impressive and fascinating way that they at once arrest the reader's attention. Practical suggestions about how to lead a really spiritual life and solutions of various intricate problems concerning different religions have been presented in such a lucid and easy style that they will be interesting and beneficial to both young and old.

Our good friends, Prof. K. Swaminathan, Prof. P. Sankaranarayanan and Prof. S. Ramaswami, have laid us under a deep debt of gratitude by translating the book into English. They have left no stone unturned to make the translation as faithful and interesting as possible.

We have priced the book nominally, so that it may reach every door.

Our labour will be amply rewarded if the

precious teachings of the Master, expounded in this book, arouse in the readers a desire to live up to them.

We are glad to announce that *Ramakrishna Upanishadam* has been considered as the best book in Tamil for the year 1952-53 in education, psychology and religion by the Tamil Academy of Madras. Sri C. Rajagopalachari has very kindly made over the Prize amount of Rs. 500/- to our Math for which we offer him our sincere thanks.

2nd October, 1953.   PUBLISHER.

PREFACE

Since I returned from Delhi some time ago, I have been writing in " Kalki ", the Tamil weekly, a series of short articles explaining the teaching of Sri Ramakrishna to the best of my understanding and ability. I wrote the first few articles with great diffidence, but friends who read them encouraged me by expressing their appreciation. Thus, by the grace of God, I had the continued happiness of writing week after week on the teachings of Bhagavan Sri Ramakrishna.

This series of thirty-five chapters was completed on Deepavali day. Thanks to the kindness of the Sri Ramakrishna Math, the idea of bringing out these articles in book form was fulfilled. It was my good fortune that the authorities of the Math approved and accepted what I wrote. As Yama Dharmaraja taught Nachiketas, the vision of the Supreme cannot be attained by the mere study of *Sastras*; nor could knowledge of the Self come through subtlety of intellect or much learning or argument. The grace of God is the one thing necessary and for that the heart should melt in *Bhakti*. *Bhakti* is different from *Sastric* learning. One may get by heart and recite without cessation the Sanskrit scriptures; one may know and repeat upside down the commentaries of the Acharyas. But righteous conduct and equanimity of mind are different and more necessary gifts. When the heart has not mellowed, study and exposition of *Sastras* are a mere

monkey game. Without wisdom in the heart, all
learning is useless. When that which is within and
that which is without are one and the same, we have
wisdom. When they are not, our learning is no
better than the tricks of a trained monkey. The
teaching of Sri Ramakrishna gives us, not mere
learning, but true wisdom. May young and old
study and profit from the teachings of Sri Ramakrishna!

15-11-1950.   C. RAJAGOPALACHARI.

CONTENTS

		PAGE
I.	GOD	1
II.	RELIGIOUS DIFFERENCES	4
III.	DON'T APPROACH THE SERPENT!	7
IV.	PURITY OF MIND	11
V.	THE WAY OF DEVOTION	14
VI.	A KING AND A BHAGAVATAR	18
VII.	WOMANHOOD AND MOTHERHOOD	21
VIII.	EVEN THE DUMB WILL SPEAK	24
IX.	THE STORY OF THE ASCETIC	28
X.	SPEECH AND SILENCE	31
XI.	OIL CUP	34
XII.	DEVI-KAVACHAM	37
XIII.	THE BOAT ON THE WATER	42
XIV.	SOCIAL SERVICE	45
XV.	NON-DUALITY (ADVAITAM)	50
XVI.	INCARNATION IN IMAGES	53
XVII.	BHAJA GOVINDAM	56
XVIII.	SOCIAL REFORM	59
XIX.	SELF-CONTROL	62
XX.	WORTH ONLY AN ANNA AND A HALF	64

		PAGE
XXI.	ROCK BOTTOM	66
XXII.	CALL AND HE WILL COME	68
XXIII.	THE CARPENTER'S WIFE	70
XXIV.	RUMINATING	72
XXV.	THE WAY TO BE SAVED	74
XXVI.	YOUR OWN MOTHER	76
XXVII.	THE DEVOTEE	79
XXVIII.	WHY STILL FALSEHOOD AND DISHONESTY?	81
XXIX.	PRAYER	82
XXX.	THE UNDYING LAMP	85
XXXI.	KAMALA'S MIRROR	86
XXXII.	SAVING ONESELF AND PREACH- ING TO OTHERS	89
XXXIII.	HAVE NO DOUBT	90
XXXIV.	ADVICE TO A GRANNY	93
XXXV.	WHERE IS GOPALA	95

SRI RAMAKRISHNA UPANISHAD

1. GOD

It is no exaggeration to call Sri Ramakrishna's teachings an Upanishad. A sage like the Rishis of old was born in our age. This was Ramakrishna Paramahamsa. He wrote no book; he made no speech. He lived a true sannyasin's life and passed away. He used to talk to his disciples who sat and listened to him with devotion. His disciples wrote down the words of their Master. This record forms his " Teachings ".

Learned men with a command of language can and do write excellent essays and discourses. But these writings lack true life. Sri Ramakrishna was a Mahatma who saw God in his heart and in all things in the world outside. He saw Him in all things with the same certainty and strength of feeling with which we see each other. Such re-markable seers have sprung in different lands from time to time.

There is a peculiar power in the words of those who lead a godly life. They have a force which the exhortations of merely learned and intellectual men do not have. When a Maharshi talks, it is his whole life that speaks through him, not mere intellect. Dialectics and exposition, however beautiful and loaded with substance, cannot compare with the spoken words of God-inspired saints.

Our society has come into its own in a political sense. To obtain happiness along with freedom, our people should tread the path of *dharma*. Thus we can secure the real joy and glory of life. Many men now assert boldly that there is no God. This is our misfortune. We see the whole world and all the wonderful objects and energies in it arising one from another. Everything goes on and revolves according to law. Can law arise by itself? All this cannot come into being except from a seed which is the first cause of all. Can any thing or any force or any law come out of nothing? Surely there must be an ultimate cause which speech and mind return from without attaining. *That* is the Supreme. To say that law is inherent in Nature and that there is no need to speak of God as its source is to substitute Nature for God. There is no point in so glorifying Nature in place of God.

True, we cannot see God; but from that can we say He does not exist? We see multitudes of stars at night; we cannot see them by day. Does " invisible " mean " non-existent "? We are finite and limited in our vision and so we are not able to see God. But for that reason let us not say, " There is no God " or " There is no need for Him".

Sri Ramakrishna said one day: " A man comes to a big city. First he fixes a place to deposit his baggage and then he goes about to see the town. After going about all day, at nightfall he goes to rest in the lodging that he has fixed. If he had not done this beforehand, he would suffer for want of a shelter in the night after his gay wandering during day. Even so, God is the rest-house for the soul wandering in the world. It is wise to secure that rest-house. Otherwise we will come to grief without joy and peace. My son, a time will come when you are enveloped by darkness after the joys of life have passed away. Then you will need a refuge to find peace. Let us realize, therefore, the need for this Refuge, that is, God."

When you immerse your pot into a tank to lift some water to drink, you do it gently to collect the clear water on the surface. You do not plunge the pot violently, stirring the water and making it muddy. If one wishes to attain purity of heart and lead a life of *dharma*, one must be steadfast in devotion and practise meditation and worship. One must not waste time or confuse the mind by pedantic discourses on sacred texts, by intellectual dialectics and theological debates. Our little intellect is like shallow water in a little pond. If we stir it too much it is the mire that comes to the top.

Everyone knows that we can get butter from curds. To get the butter, we must churn the curds. No amount of repetition of the formula " We can get butter from curds " will give us the butter. To see the Supreme, we must churn our heart's desire with devotion. It is not enough if we discourse learnedly on the Paramatma and the Jivatma. We must yearn for God even as a child yearns for its absent mother.

II. RELIGIOUS DIFFERENCES

" We can worship God in various ways and obtain His vision and grace. Are there not many *ghats* in a river? So also in the full river of bliss that is the Supreme there are many *ghats*. We can get down in any *ghat* to fetch water or to bathe. Whatever the faith we profess or the method we adopt, if we do it with pure heart and with devotion, we can attain God. One can reach the top floor of a house by getting up the stairs or one can use a bamboo ladder or one can hold on to a rope and get up by it. Similarly, our religions show several paths.

" It is proper that each person worships God according to his own religion. It is best that Christians follow Christ's way, that Muslims follow the path shown by the Prophet Muhammad and that Hindus practise the method taught by the Rishis. True devotees of any religion will honour the followers of other religions with great humility. All religions will lead us to the Supreme."

Thus did Ramakrishna Paramahamsa teach a hundred years ago. We see the same teaching in the inscription that Emperor Asoka carved on stone pillars two thousand years ago. It runs as follows:

" The Command of Devanampriya. The king honours with appropriate bounties and in other ways all ascetics and householders to whatever religion they may belong; and thus makes them happy. What pleases the King most is that men of all religions should develop their spiritual strength. One can develop one's spiritual strength by various means. But the basis of all of them is that one should resist the temptation to glorify one's own religion by speaking ill of the religion of others, and one should at every opportunity honour and exalt the men of other faiths. By doing this, one helps men of other religions and at the same time enhances the greatness of one's own religion. But, if, without doing this, a person speaks ill of other religions and belittles their votaries, he does harm to his own religion. Can a man add to the greatness of his religion by decrying another's religion? Never. Surely the good name of his faith will suffer by this. It will not increase. The followers of the several religions must learn well the tenets of their respective religions and increase their devotion by the methods prescribed by each. Let all men proclaim that this is the wish of Asoka Priyadarsana."

The message of Sri Krishna in the Bhagavad Gita thousands of years ago, the twelfth stone Edict of Emperor Asoka later, the teaching of Sri Ramakrishna Paramahamsa in the last century and the injunction of Mahatma Gandhi who was born in our time and showed us the way in various spheres,— all these are identical and equally clear. Let us understand well and follow with steadfast faith the path laid down by them.

Two boys were quarrelling with each other about the colour of a chameleon that they saw on a tree.

" Look at it carefully, that chameleon is red.

Like a blind man, you said it was yellow! " said one.

" Fool! It is you who are blind, not I. The chameleon is yellow and you say it is red! " retorted the other boy.

Thus the quarrel became hot. They then went to a hut in the garden and requested an old woman living in it to decide the issue.

The old woman asked, " What are you quarrelling about? "

The boy who had asserted that the chameleon was red, said, " Look at that tree. There is a red chameleon on it. This fellow says it is yellow. He taunts me saying I am blind. Please do look at it and tell us. This fool will accept what you say. "

The other boy broke in and said, " Mother, yes, do see it yourself. This obstinate fellow is blind and cannot see that the creature is really yellow. He thinks it is red. Red! "

The old woman laughed and said, " Both of you are right. What you see on the tree is a chameleon which can take many colours. I have often seen it change its colour. Go now, and don't quarrel."

To those who have seen and enjoyed the vision of God with the eyes of devotion, He appears in various forms. Those who cleverly dispute about religion without having seen God can never understand His true nature. They will consider their ego as their God and waste their time in vain talk and strife.

Four blind men went to beg among the servants of the head of a *Math*. There was an elephant there and they felt all over it with their hands. The mahout made fun of them and asked them, " What is the animal like? "

Touching its leg, one of the blind men said, " This animal is like a pillar."

" Tush! it is like the branch of a tree and you say it is like a pillar, " rejoined the second blind man. He had touched the elephant's trunk.

" What do you say? Is this not like a cask? " said he who felt the elephant's stomach.

" How cleverly you talk! Here is an animal which is like a winnowing fan and you compare it to a cask and to a stick and to a pillar! How you prate! " said the fourth blind man who felt the elephant's ear.

Thus limited in understanding are those who, mentally blind, quarrel about the form of the Supreme.

III. DON'T APPROACH THE SERPENT!

A big merchant once came to Paramahamsa and said, "Great one! I have settled my entire property on my family. I do not now do any business. Still God has not appeared before me. What is the reason for this? People say that one can see God if one gives up everything."

Ramakrishna replied, " Even if you pour out all the oil from an old oil pot, there will still be some oil sticking at the bottom. The oil that has soaked

in the pot for a long time cannot be poured out.
The pot cannot be cleaned and the odour will
remain. So also, traces of your worldly life cannot
be got rid of easily. You might have given away
all your properties. Yet, the attachment to the
world rooted in your heart will not go easily."

We cannot become sannyasins by merely giving
away all we have. The desire to be rid of the worry
of management may be what prompts such a step.
But it is a different matter to cut oneself free of the
bonds of wealth, relation and lust and to attain the
state of wisdom born of devotion to God.

To renounce everything without a real chastening
of the heart, then to be agitated by the constant
thought of the things renounced, and then to dis-
semble for fear of public censure—this is not true
renunciation.

Even as we take due precautions for our safety
in a snake-infested house, we must be careful how we
live in the world where lurk the venomous snakes
of lust and greed. Like a cobra that suddenly
darts out of its dark hole and bites and kills, greed
and lust quickly bring about a man's fall in an
unexpected way. The wisest of us must be ceaselessly on the alert. We must hold the thought of
God in our minds without intermission. In our
villages, in olden times, if people saw a cobra in the
house, they used to chant a mantra to say: " O
Worshipful One, turn tail and go. Go away without
raising your hood." The serpent will then go away.
Lust in the heart should be considered as a cobra.

One should not play with it. It is wise to stand at a distance from it. To think " I am wise, why need I fear? What harm will come to me from this? I shall surely keep within proper bounds. I shall go no further ", is the sign of folly. If a serpent is approached, it will surely bite.

A rich man went to Sri Ramakrishna and said, " I wish to donate a large sum of money to you. Please take this cheque and use it for meeting your expenses."

The rich man made this request from a good motive. But Sri Ramakrishna did not agree. He declined the offer and said, " No. If I accept your gift, I shall have to be thinking of it. My mind will get entangled in this wealth and will wander."

The rich man persisted and replied, " I wish to help a truly deserving person. Why do you prevent this? You need not touch the money. I wish to see you served properly. Let me invest the amount in the name of a relative of yours. Do please agree at least to this."

Sri Ramakrishna did not agree even to this. " What is the difference ", he asked, " between your second proposal and your first? Can Truth be cheated? Suppose I do not take the money directly from you, but agree to your proposal that another should take it in trust for me. Then will not my mind be occupied with the thought of how much money he received from you, how much he has now, and so on? Will I not then be always thinking of that money? No. I can never agree to any such arrangement. I don't want your money at all."

Still the rich man was insistent. He argued, " You have no attachment. Your heart is like oil floating on water. Why should the brave have any fear? You have yourself declared that even if wealth and woman's beauty are surging all around like the ocean, the pure heart will not mix with the water, but will float on it like oil."

Sri Ramakrishna smiled and replied, " The heart of a man of detachment may float like oil on water. But don't you know that even the best oil, if it has been long mixed with water, gets impure and smells foul? "

*　　*　　*　　*　　*

It is true the pure heart has great power. It can protect itself from all dangers. It will not be easily snared. But it is wrong to dally with evil for long. Even a wise man's heart will falter at times. The mark of wisdom is to keep at a distance from things which entice the heart. But if a person approaches them and yields to them step by step, even to test himself, he will surely be lost.

IV. PURITY OF MIND

When we see a beautiful woman, we must think of Devi, the Mother of the Universe. Reminding ourselves that the woman in front of us is one of the forms of the Divine Mother, we should bow down at the feet of the Mother before us, saying, " You are an incarnation of Devi. Can the Mother of the Universe be anything but beautiful? " We should become like a little child. When a child sees its mother, what other thought will enter its mind? This was the method which Sri Ramakrishna practised from the beginning. Even the wise and the learned yield to the temptations of lust. Sri Ramakrishna has thus taught a good means of escape from this danger.

We should not hate the feminine form. And we should not decry women. It is wrong to speak of women as deceitful creatures. It is not proper to hate one's mother or speak ill of her. Our mother is the Devi herself made flesh. The Devi is your mother; She is everybody's mother. She is the embodiment of Sakti. She is the Mother of the Universe. She is a form of the all-pervasive Supreme. Her beauty and her smile signify maternal tenderness. Bow before the Devi. Your lust will vanish. Practise this method taught by Bhagavan Ramakrishna. You will immediately discover that your mind becomes ever purer.

A pot and a ladle do not constitute food, though they may be used to cook and serve your food.

Reading a list of things you want will not bring them before you. Teaching will avail nothing unless you exert yourself. Turn your mind to the practice of devotion.

When your mind falters at the sight of the beautiful form of a woman, think then of Sita who did penance under a tree in Asokavana. Will you join the rakshasas or will you fall at the feet of Hanuman, confess the hidden weakness in your mind and pray for the grace of the Mother? Standing in the form of the woman before you, the Devi demands your pure devotion. Do not yield to your passion like a fool. Do not seek your own destruction, mistaking the false for the true.

The springs of good and evil are both in our mind. The thoughts which arise in it transform themselves into external acts. Do not let your mind become by degrees a dirty pool in the belief that the overt action alone matters and that no one will know what passes in the mind. Otherwise, all your life's actions will become evil beyond redemption, as surely as the health of a whole village will be spoiled if filth gathers in the village well.

Once two friends were walking aimlessly along a street. They saw someone in a house reading a Purana and a gathering of devotees listening to the exposition.

Said Tiruvengadam, " Come along! We shall also go in and listen to the story."

Samban replied, " I do not at all like this story-telling. What is the use of this? These people waste their time in mere fiction. There is the street of the harlots. Let us go there and let us spend the night pleasantly there. Our troubles are always with us. May we not spend one day in pleasure? "

Tiruvengadam did not agree with Samban. He said, " I don't want all that. If you wish, you had better go. I shall sit down here and listen to the story." The friends parted. Samban went to the harlots' street. Tiruvengadam joined the group listening to the religious discourse.

Somehow, Samban did not feel happy in the harlot's house. He felt sad and mused to himself, " Why did I come here and get stuck up here? Would it not have been well if I too had gone to listen to the Purana? " Four others were there playing cards and talking joyfully. He joined them. But his mind was not there. He was thinking of the house where the *harikatha* was going on.

As for Tiruvengadam, though he was among those listening to the discourse, his mind was not in the story. He was observing that the Bhagavatar did not sing well and that his voice was hoarse. He did not feel drawn to the story. "What will Samban be doing now? How happy must he be now? It would have been well if I too had gone with him." The thought of Samban and the revelry in the harlot's house engaged Tiruvengadam's mind.

Though Samban was in the harlot's house, his mind was there where the Purana was being expounded. He spent his night thinking, " How happy must Tiruvengadam be now! He is acquiring spiritual merit while I am in the midst of these fools here! "

In fact, though Tiruvengadam stayed amidst devotees, as his mind was not pure, he was guilty of the sin of going to a harlot's house. Though Samban was in a harlot's house, as his mind was intent on the gathering of devotees, in a measure he became pure. Though he went to a house of ill fame, he saved himself from destruction by purity of mind.

V. THE WAY OF DEVOTION

Bhagavan Ramarksihna tells a pupil: You see me in front of you. But if I hold a cloth before my face you do not see me. At once I am hidden. Yet, I am near you as before. But, hidden behind the cloth, I become non-existent to your eyes. In this way, God is near you and me and everyone. He is nearer to us than all other things. But the curtain of the ego (the " I ") hides Him. If you hold even a small piece of cloth before your eyes, even a big mountain is hidden from your view. We cannot see God as long as we hold before us the curtain of egotism and pride. If the " I " disappears, God will appear in all His brightness.

If a person is dowered with grace, he will realise that all his actions are God's and that whatever happens is the sport of that great artist in play, God. When he realises this, he becomes a *jivanmukta*, that is, he attains salvation in this body before he dies. He has no fear, no sorrow.

An earnest devotee frequently reminds himself, " Oh Lord! It is you that do everything. There is nothing that I can do. I am but a plaything in your hands. It is you who make me do things. Everything is your glory. If I do anything well, it is your glory. This house and this family are not mine. They are yours. I am your servant obeying your will. To obey you and serve you is my right and my delight."

Reminding ourselves thus, if we lead our lives with true devotion, the curtain of the " I " will disappear and we shall see a glorious sight.

This " I " is of two kinds. One is the feeling of " I " as a result of mature devotion. The other immature pride. This latter is associated with thoughts like " my house, my child, my wife, my body, my property, etc." This is the curtain that hides God from us.

The devotee leads his life telling himself, " I seek to serve the will of God. All that is His, His right, His glory. I am His servant. Serving Him is my great delight." By a life of this kind, pride ripens and falls off. The devotee becomes a *jivan-mukta*.

But the thought of " I " cannot be easily got rid of. Intelligence and a knowledge of Advaita will not suffice. Man should convert himself completely into a servant of God and live accordingly. The devotee's " I " (Ego) is not impure. It is as sinless as a child's ego. It is the unripe " I " that must be destroyed. The devotee's feeling of " I " will lead him to God. Even if there is a trace of the ego in the heart of him who treads the path of devotion, it lies there as the slave of God. That does not matter. The way of devotion is a noble path.

*　　*　　*　　*　　*

Though we wash it many times, a vessel which contained garlic always retains its smell. Egoism is also like that. It is a wicked quality. Many perhaps may or may not succeed in getting rid of it. But for a recluse, if the ego is gently led into the path of devotion and steadily corrected, then it will ripen and fall off and disappear.

*　　*　　*　　*　　*

A learned physician once came to see an ailing child and told the mother, " Don't be anxious. I shall cure the child. I shall be responsible for the child's life."

Sri Ramakrishna says that God laughs when a physician talks thus. The true guardian and master of life is God, not the physician. Every life is in the hands of God.

Deciding that they could not any longer live as a joint family, two brothers prepared to partition their lands. The elder brother took hold of a tape,

measured the lands and told his brother, " This
is your land and that is mine." Says Sri Ramakrishna, "God laughs at such fools. What can God
do but laugh at a man saying, ' This thing is
mine,'—when he himself is but a helpless, transient
creature?"

Years ago, in a country in the West, there was a
young Christian monk. He lived in a monastery
and spent his time cooking for the monks and in
serving them in other ways. He was not a learned
man. He was also young. Yet, he was a devotee
with a pure heart. Whatever he did, cooking,
washing clothes or cleaning pots, he did as a service
to God Himself. He had no time or place for
prayer or meditation. He felt that God was always
beside him when he was doing any work anywhere.
God became his constant companion. He found
that God was ever with him, sleeping with him,
playing with him and working with him. To the
other monks in the monastery, his devoted and
constant cheerfulness was a perpetual wonder.
When we read all this of Brother Lawrence, we are
reminded of the story of the gopis of Brindavan and
of the life of Sri Ramakrishna. In every country,
in every age, there have been mahatmas, *jivan-
muktas*, who have seen God face to face.

3

VI. A KING AND A BHAGAVATAR

A Brahmin, learned in the Sastras and the Puranas, went to a king and told him that he desired to read and expound the Puranas in the palace. The Brahmin said, " Maharaj! The Bhagavata is a great book of *dharma*. You must study it under a good teacher. If you command me, I shall expound it to you. I am known to scholars as a great Pandit learned in the Dharma Sastras. I long to read and expound the Bhagavata in the palace."

The king was a shrewd man with sound common sense. He said to himself: " If this man had read and understood the true import of the Bhagavata, he would be performing meditation and austerity. He would not have come to royal palaces in quest of money and fame." Addressing the Brahmin, he said: " Learned one! I too am eager to make you my teacher and hear your expositon of the Bhagavata. So, read the work again once or twice, and come later."

The scholar was somewhat angry when he heard what the king said. But what was the use of getting angry with a king? He returned home without uttering a word. As he walked home, he said to himself in grief: " This king is a great fool. He cannot recognize a learned man. He asks me to go back to him after reading the Bhagavata again! I have spent twelve years in reading the Sastras. I have got the whole of the Bhagavata by heart. And this king wants me to read it again! "

Coming home, he told his wife what had happened. After thinking for a while, she said: "After all he is a king. Do as he bids you. Read the Bhagavata once again and then go to him and tell him that you have done his bidding. If you should please the king somehow and get appointed as the palace story-teller, our fortune is made."

The Brahmin took his wife's advice and read the Bhagavata again with great care. He was now able to answer any question on the work. On an auspicious day he went to the palace again.

The king received the Brahmin with great respect. To the king's query if he had re-read the Bhagavata, the Brahmin replied: "Your Majesty! I have come here after reading the Purana again a number of times as your Majesty commanded. My only desire is that I should expound the Bhagavata to you and help to enhance your glory and righteousness!"

Said the king: "O learned one! Be assured that I shall be your student and learn the Bhagavata from you. But, go home now and return after reading the work once again."

Thus disappointed again, the Brahmin returned home and told his wife what had happened. She said to him: "There is some mystery in this. Read it once again as the king said. Let us see."

With great perseverance, the Pandit began to read again. Determined not to be disappointed this time, he went to a solitary abode and read the book with great attention and deep concentration.

This time, he discovered new meanings in the work.
The glory of God's incarnation moved his heart in
spite of himself. He even forgot to take his food in
time. He found rare truths in the Bhagavata which
he had not discovered before. He had no thought
even of going home.

He now realized that fame, money and honour
are but flies. After a time, he even ceased to read
the Bhagavata. He spent his time in meditation.
He gave up all idea of going to the king's palace.

While thus he spent his time in meditation
and penance, without attending to the household,
his wife was puzzled and grieved by the turn of
events. She asked for leave to see the king and
conveyed her anguish to him. The king, on learning
what had happened, was mightily pleased. He
started to go and see the Brahmin himself.

When he came to the Ashrama, the king saw a
new lustre in the Brahmin's countenance. The light
of supreme wisdom shone bright in his face.

The king fell at the Brahmin's feet, and said:
"You have won the grace of God. I bow to you.
Forgive my sin."

Learning and scholarship are quite different from
true wisdom, the knowledge of the Real, which
comes only through devotion.

VII. WOMANHOOD AND MOTHERHOOD

Bhagavan Ramakrishna constantly regarded all women as embodiments of the Devi. The Devi manifests Herself in women. The women that you see are so many aspects or forms of the Divine Mother. So, when you see any of them, you must fill your mind with reverence like one going into the shrine of the Devi Herself and feel that the Devi is giving *darshan* to you through that woman. Regard all women as the Devi's forms and bow to them, whether those women are good-natured or evil-natured. You and I have no right to censure or praise them. We cannot understand the cosmic play of the Devi which has called the world into being. Our duty is to bow humbly to Her will. All women are the Devi's forms. You adore the decorated image of the Devi in the shrine. These women are the living forms of the same Devi. You must bow to them as well.

"Gurudev! How should we conduct ourselves before womankind?" asked a disciple of the Paramahamsa.

"He who has had *darshan* of God by His grace need have no fears about women. He will look on all women as images of our common Mother. He will realize that the great Devi manifests Herself in the various women he sees around him and he will worship them as such. He will worhsip them with love and devotion as he worships his own mother."

" Gurudev! How can I overcome lust? Teach me that."

" I am telling you that. Regard every woman you see as your own mother. Bow down at her feet and make obeisance. Then evil thoughts will vanish from your mind."

*   *   *   .   *   *

" Though married and living with their husbands, some women lead a virgin's life. They are visible embodiments of the Devi."

A disciple asked Sri Ramakrishna: " Following the Tantric way, some persons worship the Devi in the company of women devotees. Do you approve of that? "

In Bengal and certain other places, some people follow the Sakta form of worship. There are also evil men among them. It was about these men that the disciple put this question. Sri Ramakrishna uttered a warning in these terms:

" This is a dangerous method. Ordinary men should not adopt it. Following this very difficult path, one may be led into sin. Considering a woman as Sakti and worshipping her as such is a part of the Tantric mode of worship. This can be done in three ways. First, the devotee may consider himself as a son. He worships a woman with such affection and respect as a son shows to his mother. Second, the devotee may consider himself as a woman-friend or companion and worship her with that attitude.

" Of these two, the worship of the Devi as one's mother—to remain steadfast in that attitude and to lose oneself in it—is the superior way. To look on Her as a friend and worship Her as such is also good.

" There is a third way. That is the bride-bridegroom attitude. This is a dangerous method. It must not be followed."

In the Tantras, there is described a method of worshipping in secret a living woman as the Devi in the same way as we worship an image in a temple. The Paramahamsa prohibits this. Speaking about his own experience, he says: " I have spent two years in this Tantric practice. I practised the attitude of friend and of child. I found the attitude of a child to its mother most congenial. I have never worshipped the Devi looking on Her as my spouse. It is a difficult method indeed. I would forbid it altogether."

Some one asked Bhagavan, " Why don't you lead a householder's life with your wife? " He told a story by way of answer:

" One day, Ganesa, Paramasiva's son, scratched a cat with his nails. Later he went to his mother and saw scratches on her cheek. ' How did you get these scratches, mother? ' he asked. ' Who has hurt you thus? '

Parvati replied, ' Child, you have done this. You scratched my face with your nails.'

' How is this, mother? When did I scratch you? ' asked Ganesa.

'Darling! Have you forgotten what you did to the cat?' said Gauri.

Ganesa asked: 'Yes. I did scratch the cat. But why do the scratches appear on your cheek?'

The mother replied, 'Child, don't you know that the whole world is my body? If any one hurts any living creature, he hurts me.'

"After this Ganesa could marry none. Every woman he saw appeared to him as his mother. Womankind signified the Divine Mother to him. So he gave up all thought of marriage. Even so, to my eyes too, every woman looks to be Parvati Herself. What can I do?"

VIII. EVEN THE DUMB WILL SPEAK

One day Keshab Chandra Sen, one of the leaders of the Brahma Samaj, visited Sri Ramakrishna at the Dakshineswar temple.

"Why do even learned scholars behave foolishly sometimes? Though learned in the Sastras, they seem to lack wisdom. They wallow in pleasure, clinging to their desires," said Keshab Chandra.

Ramakrishna Paramahamsa replied, "Eagles fly in the sky. They fly high aloft in the pure regions of the sky. Yet, their eyes are fixed on the carcass, flesh and bones on the ground."

Even while we read the holy texts, our minds

tend to wander away to the things we desire. Learning is one thing. The objects we desire are another. Our attempts to get wise by study of holy books are hindered by our desires and attachments.

Learning alone will not be of much use. We may have a command of language. We may recite holy verses. We may chant mantras correctly. That is all. It is the things that we desire, that raise us or debase us. All the learning that we gain from books will not give us wisdom or salvation so long as we let ourselves be entangled by woman, wealth and worldly objects. Learning may help us to give learned discourses. Talking about Brahman, the Supreme, Jnana-yoga, Bhakti-yoga, primordial matter, Jivatma and Paramatma, we may fill our listeners with wonder. But our talk proceeds from the lips only. It does not flow from the heart. We shall reap the benefit of our scholarship only if our heart is touched and our mind turned to God. Otherwise, the Sastras and Puranas will avail nothing. We may utter the names of notes of music sa, ri, ga, ma, pa, dha, ni. But the notes in isolation are not music. It is easy to make a discourse on wisdom and renunciation by arranging words in correct sequence. But a life of real wisdom and strict renunciation is a different and a very difficult thing indeed.

We find it stated in an almanac that there will be a certain amount of rain on a particular day. This may also come true. But we cannot get rain-water by pressing the leaves of the almanac with

our hands.   You may press your hardest, you will
not get a drop of water.   You may find many noble
sentiments in the scriptures.   But one cannot attain
devotion merely by reading them.   If there is control
of one's desires as prescribed in them, devotion will
then arise.

In the presence of God, of what avail are learning
and intellect?   There even the dumb will speak
and the blind will see.   To God, the learned and the
unlettered are all one.

Merely crying out " opium " even a hundred
times will not intoxicate you.   Intoxication will
arise only if a little opium is taken in the hand,
pounded, dissolved in water and consumed.   There
is no use in uttering the thousand names of God
without turning the mind to Him.   One must
practise meditation after concentrating the mind
with steadfastness.   Then only can the Supreme
be seen.

*   *   *   *   *

A man talking to others about the Supreme after
reading the Sastras is like one who, after seeing the
dot indicating Banaras on a map, says " I have seen
Banaras".   Cities, rivers and hills are marked
accurately on a map.   But to see them on the map
is not the same as actually seeing them.   A ball
of thread sometimes gets ravelled.   We cannot use
it unless the knot is unravelled.   Even so, words in
books become knotty.   Involved in them, we are not
able to find a way out, unless we have devotion,

virtue and meditation. Without humility and devotion and without God's grace, all the books that a man reads will only increase the evil in his nature. His learning serves but to make his ego bigger and prevents the dawn of wisdom in his mind.

Egotism is like a heap of ashes. All the water poured on it will be just absorbed by it. Unless one melts in devotion to God, egotism will not vanish. All the Sanskrit one learns, all the thinking that one does will be like water poured on a heap of ashes. The sacred books only point the way to the Supreme. Without virtue, devotion and meditation, they cannot help one to reach It.

We take to a shop a list of things that we wish to buy. When once we know what we wish to buy, the list becomes useless. The Sastras declare the way to attain God. Knowing the way, our only duty is to pursue it. If we merely think about a list of articles, the things will not come into our hands. To go to a town we must not only know the way, we must walk along it. It is not enough to know the way. We can reach the town only if we walk on that way.

When Sri Chaitanya was going on a pilgrimage in the south, he saw a scholar discoursing on the Gita. There was a devotee among the audience who knew not the meaning of even a single verse in the Gita. Yet, all through the discourse, tears were flowing copiously from his yes.

Sri Chaitanya asked him, " Dear one! Why do you weep? What ails you? "

The devotee replied, " I see Sri Krishna and Arjuna on the chariot. At the sight of them, tears flow down my eyes. Not a word of the discourse enters my ears."

This illiterate devotee was a man of true wisdom. The meaning and purpose of all the Sastras is to give us this intense love of God.

IX. THE STORY OF THE ASCETIC

An ascetic lived in a house near a temple. There was a harlot in the house opposite. Every day he saw men visiting her. The ascetic was filled with grief that so many men led such vicious lives. One day he called the harlot and reproved her: " Sinful one! Day and night you lead this evil life. What will you do when Death comes? "

These words touched her mind. She grieved over her lot and began to pray to God. " O God, " said she in anguish, " save me from my sins." She prayed to God every day. But she had no other means of livelihood. And so, she pursued her profession as before.

Night and day she implored God and said, " Alas! Knowing no other means of earning my livelihood, I lead this sinful life. Save me, O God?"

The ascetic said to himself: " Well, my advice seems to be in vain. She does not give up her trade. Let me see, let me keep a count of the number of men that visit her."

From that day, the ascetic was intent on counting the number of persons who visited her house. He used little pebbles to keep count of the number. As the days passed, the heap of pebbles rose higher and higher. One day, he called the harlot and pointing to the heap, said to her, " Look at this heap of stones. They are a measure of your sins. Unmindful of my counsel, you have stuck to your trade. This heap shows the sin you have committed despite my warning. Know from this the torments that await you. How can you hope for salvation? Begone! "

The harlot trembled when she saw the heap of pebbles. " O God, " said she, " What shall I do? " With fear and trembling she went home. Unable to bear her grief, she began to cry. " O Krishna, " she called out, " pray, lift me up and save me from my sins. Take, if you will, my life. " So saying, she fell down unconscious.

God took mercy on that poor woman. She died that night.

The ascetic too died the same night. His life passed out of his body.

Wonder of wonders! Yama's servants dragged the ascetic's soul to hell; but the soul of the harlot who repented for her sins went to Vishnu's abode.

The ascetic saw the harlot's soul on its heavenward journey, and cried out: " You, Harlot! how can you go to heaven? You have committed innumerable sins. The pebbles with which I counted them rose to a big heap. As for me, I was a pure ascetic. I never committed a sin. Consigning me to hell, God takes you to heaven. This God does not seem to know Dharma! "

Vishnu's messengers pacified the ascetic, and said, " O man, do not excite yourself. God does not falter in His wisdom. Your life was but an outward show. When you put on the garb of an ascetic, you were after show and fame. Look, there lies your earthly body. It was pure indeed. And so, men deck it with flowers and carry it to the accompaniment of music. The body which you kept pure has been duly honoured. But you go to hell. The body of this harlot committed many sins. Look, vultures peck at it and prey on it. No one cares even to cremate it. But her soul was pure, and so we carry it to God's presence. You counted, didn't you?, the harlot's sins. As you busied yourself about her sins, their pollution clings to you. Her heart which took refuge in God and grieved over her sins was freed from taint and became pure. You who counted her sins carry them on your head."

It is no part of a devotee's work to count the sins of others. Who can understand the sport of God? He leads us and He tests us. The good and evil in us, He alone can know and judge. One should keep one's heart steadfast in purity and look at the faults of others with a kindly eye.

X. SPEECH AND SILENCE

One who has attained wisdom by devotion and good conduct and with the grace of God will be an example to others even though he may not speak to them. Only those who have known God through love can reach this state. A knowledge of the scriptures is not enough. A person who has only read of the snow on the Himalays or heard of it from others cannot speak of it clearly to others. Only those who have seen it, touched it with their hands and tasted it will have the knowledge and the right to speak of it to others.

A devotee who says, "I have understood the state of salvation. I intend to preach it to others and I shall gather a group of disciples about me" is clearly an egotist. Whoever is chosen by God will automatically get the power to teach. To seek to teach without the authority of God is to display fruitless egotism.

When flowers are filled with honey, bees settle on them of their own accord. There is no need to invite ants to a place where there is jaggery. If a man has attained real wisdom and if his life is governed by it, there is no need to call people to him. His wisdom will flow on all sides like a flood of nectar and all will turn to him of themselves. The sweetness that attracts ants and bees should exist in the recesses of the heart. In God's creation, purity of mind is like jaggery, sweet. The pure soul will draw disciples to itself, as a magnet draws iron.

Thoes who have not received the grace of God preach in vain. Their words will not penetrate the heart of anyone. Only if one obtains the authority of God by one's devotion and virtue can one get disciples and function as a teacher. Without God's grace all one's efforts are in vain.

When a bright light burns, swarms of insects gather from somewhere and fall into it. Nobody sends for them. Men of true wisdom are like a burning lamp. Their radiance will draw disciples to them. We cannot say from where they come.

*   *   *   *   *

All that a teacher who has attained God's grace says or does will be a form of worship of his God. All that he says or does will constitute his preaching. Preaching in the usual sense is not necessary. If a man sees God in his heart and keeps his mind steady in the thought of God, that itself will serve as his teaching. The effort that he makes to liberate himself from family ties will itself be his message to others. Like a flower which blossoms, his soul filled with honey will attract the bees and give them food.

Have you seen grain measured out and sold from a big granary? The man will measure it out without ceasing. As he measures the grain, it will slide down from the store and fall into a heap. That is the way a Guru teaches. He measures out grain from God's big granary. Wisdom and teaching flow down from it. The grain which is measured out is God's. But unlike the stocks of grain in a retail shop, the stock of God's wisdom in a pure soul is inexhaustible. This is the difference between the teaching from mere knowledge of scriptures and that which arises from the grace of God. There is no quantitative limit to the teaching which comes from God's grace. In the teaching from knowledge of texts, the stock runs out soon.

When it rains, the water flows down in full from a terrace. Outlets are fashioned like the mouth of a cow or of a tiger. When water flows through them, it looks as if it comes out of the cow's mouth or tiger's mouth. Truly, it is the rain from the sky that flows through these outlets. The precepts of wise men are like the rain from the sky. The grace of God flows through the lips of blessed teachers.

When a pot is being filled from a tank, a gurgling sound is heard. But when the pot is full the sound ceases. Those who only read the Sastras will talk much. Those who have attained wisdom enjoy God's vision in silence and are immersed in that blissful experience.

When guests are gathered at a feast, there is a great chatter among them. They are all talking to one another. But the moment they begin to eat, the noise stops. When the preparations are being served, noise gets less. When *payasam* is served, the dining hall is silent. The only sound that is heard is that of the drinking of the *payasam* by the guests. When they have finished eating, they go to the pial and sleep.

4

Discussion looms large only before one sees God. When God has been seen, there is no more need of speech.

Outside a fair there is a great deal of noise. It is the confused noise of the fair. But if we get into the fair, we do not notice the noise. We are intent on asking about the prices of things and striking a bargain. That is the way of devotion also. When we are at a distance, the noise of discussion assails our ears. When we approach God and stand in His presence, the noise of discussion is stilled and we merge in God.

There is much sound when the cake is fried in ghee in a pan. When it is well baked, there is no more sound. Devotees talk a good deal in the beginning. Speech becomes less and less as wisdom matures.

XI. OIL CUP

Once egoism entered the Sage Narada's heart. He imagined that there was no devotee like him. Knowing this, the Lord said to him: " O Narada! Go down to the earth. There is a great devotee of Mine there. Get to know him and his virtues and come back. It will do you good."

" Well, " said Narada to himself, " I shall do as the Lord bids me. I shall go and find out what special virtues that devotee has. Can there be a greater devotee than myself? Let me see this wonder." Narada then went down to the earth.

He saw a farmer in a certain house. Soon after getting up in the morning, the farmer uttered the name of Hari once and went to his field carrying his plough on his shoulder. He laboured the whole day in the field and then returned home. Again before going to bed, he uttered Hari's name.

Narada saw all this and exclaimed, " So, this man is a greater devotee than I, is he? " and laughed within himself. He waited to see what the man did the next day. The farmer uttered Hari's name again on getting up, then went to his field and, after toiling the whole day, came home and, after uttering God's name once, went to bed. " Is this all? " thought Narada, and returned to Vishnu's heaven.

Addressing Vishnu, Narada said, " I have seen your devotee. He does not seem to me to be such a great devotee. His mind is absorbed in his work in the field. You seem to have sent me to him only to make fun of me! "

Vishnu replied, " O Narada, take this cup in your hand." The sage received the oil cup that God gave him.

Vishnu added, " This cup is brimful of oil. Take care! Take this with you and go round the earth once. See that while you go round, not even a drop of oil is spilt."

Narada did as the Lord told him. He came back triumphant, taking care not to spill even a drop.

" So, you have come back. That is good, but tell me, please, how often did you think of me when you went round the world? " asked the Lord.

"O God! How could I think of You? You bade me go round without spilling even a drop of this oil. That was hard enough for me," said Narada.

"Sage, you were unable to think of me as all your thoughts were fixed on this oil cup. If that is the plight of a Jnani like you, consider the position of that poor farmer. Bearing the heavy burden of his family, does he not utter my name at least twice a day? Do you now understand the quality of his devotion?" said the Lord. And Narada · felt ashamed rather than proud of himself.

*   *   *   *   *

If the mind is caught up by the enticements of sex and wanders about, or if we are lost in sensuous desires, we must cry halt and turn the mind to good thoughts. This effort may be futile at first. Then we must seek God's aid, looking on Him as our friend or father or mother, utter His name and beseech Him to save us from our sins. We must keep Devi before our mind's eye and bow to Her as we would to our mother. Uttering the names of Rama, Vasudeva, Govinda will help us.

To wash out the impurities of the mind, the various names of the Lord will help us like so many life-giving medicines.

Some one once said to the Paramahamsa, "I do not feel any joy in recounting the names of the Lord, why?" The Paramahamsa replied: "My man, pray to God. Weep before Him and pray: 'Give me the joy of recounting your name." God will fulfil your prayer. 'My Mother, My Father, O Krishna, Rama, Sita, Gopala, Govinda, Mahadeva, O Lord Siva,' any of these names will do. Keep uttering that name every day. By degrees you will find sweetness in it. When you are ill, you do not find your food palatable at first. Gradually you feel a taste for it. That is a sign of the cure."

God and His name are not different from each other. You know that Sri Krishna was weighed. Seated on one pan of the balance was Krishna. Rukmini placed a *tulasi* leaf and the Lord's name on the other which now was lower than the pan with Krishna himself on it. As Chaitanya said, " The Lord's name is like a seed. The seed that lies on a pillar in a palace may lie idle there for many years. The building may fall down in ruins. Then that seed will fall on the ground and get into the soil. When rain falls on it, it will sprout into a plant and grow into a tree laden with flowers and fruit. God's name will never go in vain."

XII.   DEVI-KAVACHAM

The sap pervades the tree from the root to the topmost branch. It appears transformed into leaf and branch, into flower and fruit. Even so, the same ultimate Principle appears as many things in the universe. This supreme Principle pervading all creation, our great men called by various names,

such as Energy or Maya. The things that we see
and the forces around us are only the manifold trans-
formations of the supreme Principle that is present
everywhere. All living beings that are born, grow
and decay are the manifestations of that great Power.
The one Supreme, which was alone, of its own will,
separated into the many. These things thus
separated strive to become One again. That is the
root cause of the forces of attraction, physical and
mental, that we perceive. The affinity of the
separate elements, their desire to unite, is one of the
forces of attraction, which scientists have examined
and analyzed. The gravitational pull by the earth
on objects separated from it and the numerous orbs
revolving by cosmic gravitation are all the sport of
the Divine Force. Scientists have probed into the
working of this universal gravitation and tried to
explain it. That is a great part of the science of
mathematics. But the nature of that attraction, the
laws governing it, the reality of which this is an
appearance, these are all beyond their research.
That is the same Supreme Being which Sri Ramakrishna worshipped as Mahasakti, Durga and
Devi and adored with intense devotion in his
heart. She whom Sri Sankara worshipped, calling
Her by a thousand names, is the self same Mahasakti.

Among the several forms of this force of Mahasakti
the attraction of the sexes is one. We all know
that this is a sore trial to mankind. This natural
force which is the gift of Parasakti also gives
limitless delight to men. And alongside of it,

it also causes them much anguish. Family life and
the joy that springs and grows in it, are the benefits
of this force of attraction. It is also the source of
many hardships, sorrows and sins. This attraction
which is a great force was known in olden times as
our " animal nature ". It is a natural force common
to all living beings. It is no use decrying it. That
it should be controlled and directed along righteous
paths is the precept of our great teachers. Family
life and the pure love of wife and children are the
great means organized by society to canalize this
force of attraction along pure paths. If men's
animal nature strays into impure paths avoiding the
way of purity, it will surely do them great harm and
cause them much sorrow.

Some great men acquire complete mastery over
it and, converting it into soul force, remain absolutely
continent in the state of *brahmacharya*. By the grace
of Mahasakti, the whole force of their animal nature
functions as manure to their body and soul and raises
them to a lofty state. Even if one cannot completely
control it, yet one's soul force increases and the
intellect blossoms to the extent to which one forgets or
conquers one's animal nature.

*   *   *   *   *

We Tamils possess as our birthright a native good-
ness and social culture. We have inherited a keen
mind and an optimistic and joyful nature. The
emotion of the Tamils does not run riot, but flowers

into controlled and balanced conduct. In the midst of all these virtues, the attracting force of animal nature is a danger which threatens them all. If this force which is common to beasts and men is not controlled and brought under sway, it becomes a raging demon. It clouds the understanding, ruins values and works havoc on the individual and society. We must take care not to give room to this evil. Else, all the virtues of our society will be destroyed and devoured by this devil. It is only when the women of a country are able to go alone along the streets, shops and other places without fear of molestation that the society can be considered to be cultured. This is the test of a high civilization. This is an indispensable condition of a good life. On the streets of Madras are seen all degrees of civilization. Now more than ever before, men and women of all ranks put on good and tidy clothes and go out. But if we look at the ways of men, we sometimes doubt if they have brought under control their animal nature. It is natural for women to be shy in the presence of men. But shyness is one thing; fear is quite another. Why do our women feel any fear in the presence of men, their own brethren? If men's thoughts and feelings are pure, there will be no need for women to be afraid of them. Looks reveal the impulses of the heart. It is when they look at the signs visible in men's faces and eyes that women become afraid of them. What shall we think of a society in which its women are afraid of its men? Unless men subdue their animal nature, we shall have to conclude that our society is not yet properly cultured. I hope no one will be offended by my candour.

Even as Sri Ramakrishna regarded every woman that he saw as an incarnation of Devi, every one of us should think likewise and subdue our animal instincts. Bhagavan Ramakrishna looked upon even notorious prostitutes as manifestations of Durga Devi. Even when he saw a harlot, there arose in his heart the love and devotion that he would feel towards his mother. If we wish to keep out this animal nature from our heart, we should adopt Sri Ramakrishna's method. There is nothing that persistent effort cannot accomplish. Sita, Parvati, Lakshmi, Gauri, Iswari, Amba,—all these are Devi's names. When we see a woman's form, let us think of Sri Ramakrishna and with Devi's names in our heart and voice, let us say to ourselves: " This is Devi Herself; she too is the incarnation of Parasakti; let me bow to her in my heart." With that thought let us serve society and ourselves. Sri Ramakrishna has given us this Devi-Kavacha to help us lead a pure life and acquire a high culture. Let us make good use of it.

*   *   *   *   *

Young people at school and college should learn this lesson most of all. Purity of mind is the most important thing. Purity is not confined to body or clothing. The one thing necessary is to prevent one's animal nature from getting hold of one's mind. Learn to keep the mind absolutely pure. Pictures, stories and books that represent the animal nature tend to corrupt our culture. In our society there are now many facilities for men who exploit the force of animal nature and make the false appear as true. Our youths are indeed sound at heart. If we rouse their animal nature, we shall lead them to sin and degrade our society. Let us worship Parasakti, let us exalt life in the family, let us make sure that in our land any girl can move about anywhere at any time without fear and that every young man is her brother and protector. May virtue flourish in our land!

XIII.   THE BOAT ON THE WATER

The boat floats on the water. But water should not be allowed to get into the boat. If it does, the boat will sink. That is also the state of devotees who live in the world. But the world should not be allowed to get into the mind. I it does, the mind will sink into the mire of this world.

Lead a family life. Attend to your duties as a householder, but think of God all the while. When you are not preoccupied with household work, you must concentrate on God with your whole mind and soul.

A good wet-nurse suckles her mistress's infant and brings it up with affection. Though she does this as if the infant were her own, she does her duty by it,

knowing " this child is not mine, it will be nothing
to me when it grows up; suckling it is all the
connection between me and this child". The true
devotee should regard family life even as the wet-
nurse does the child entrusted to her.

What is the kind of feeling in her heart when a
maid-servant refers to the house she serves in as
" our house "? Her own house is somewhere else
in the village. She works in the town. She refers
to the house of her mistress as " our house". She
takes up her mistress's babe, fondles it saying " my
darling", " my Gopal is a mischievous child", " my
Gopal is hungry". That is how she speaks of the
child with words of love and affection. But when
she speaks thus, she does not forget that Gopal is her
mistress's child, not hers, that her child is in her place
with its grandmother. Even so should devotees in
family life go through their family duties with the
attitude of the servant maid.

*   *   *   *   *

Your home is God's house. Cultivate the thought
that God is its owner and lead your family life
accordingly. If that thought takes root, it will
become a settled mode of your mind. Those who
seek to reach God leading a family life are like soldiers
fighting from behind the ramparts of a fort. Those
who follow God abandoning the world are like
soldiers fighting on the open field. Both these kinds
of men are certainly good soldiers. Those who

fight from inside the fort have an advantage. There is nothing wrong in it.

You have seen, (haven't you?) soldiers practising on the rifle range before they fight in the open. Similarly family life is the practising ground for detachment. The advantage of living in the family is that it helps you to practise renunciation, while enjoying the conveniences of the family. Treat the family life as a gymnasium for strengthening and purifying your mind.

If you give up the family quarrelling with your father or wife and turn an ascetic, that will not be true Sannyas. That will be " sour grapes " Sannyas. It will not last long. Very soon the thoughts of such a Sannyasi will turn to old things and he will become a householder again.

Those ascetics alone will benefit by their renunciation who go through their life's duties properly and with devotion as obligations to God, train their minds to think of it all as service to God and who, with hearts so purified, renounce the world. Such men will realize the truth that all things that are, are manifestations of the Supreme.

There was a rest-house in a village where ascetics used to go and take food. One day when going round the village for alms, one of the ascetics saw a Zamindar thrashing his servant. The ascetic pitied the servant and going to the master in all humility begged him, ' Sir, stop this beating for my sake. The Lord will bless you for it.' But the Zamindar grew only more angry. Letting the servant go, he thrashed the ascetic till he fell unconscious on the ground. The Zamindar, his fury abated, went into his house.

Some passers-by who saw the ascetic lying on the ground, after pitying him, conveyed news of it to the rest-house. The other ascetics ran to the spot, lifted up the victim and carried him to the rest-house. They sprinkled cold water on his face and revived him and one of them gave him some milk to drink. After some time, the ascetic gained consciousness. Then, one of the ascetics asked him, " Brother, do you recognize me? "

" Brother, oh, yes. I know you. You beat me first and now you pour milk into my mouth."

The ascetic had attained true knowledge. He could not see any difference between the man who had beaten him and the man who had restored him. Good and evil, joy and sorrow, are but the sport of the Lord.

XIV. SOCIAL SERVICE

One day some young men came to the Parama-hamsa and said to him: " We have decided to engage ourselves in social service."

Sri Ramakrishna addressed these enthusiasts thus:

" Your decision is indeed laudable. It is good to engage in social service. But first worship God, meditate on Him and purify your heart and then take to social work. If you think of God, you will get an access of strength. If you pray to God with devotion, you will acquire the capacity to do good. Through God's grace you will get the skill and the facilities to do your work well. Pray to God constantly. Sing the songs His lovers have sung in His praise. Then you will know how to do social work well."

*　　*　　*　　*　　*

Every patriot who wishes to do social service must take note of this important teaching of Sri Rama-krishna: "Do not, from an excess of desire to work for social welfare, wander about in search of things to do, saying to yourselves, 'We shall do this, we shall do that.' Engage yourselves in the work that is at hand. Seeking for fame and name, do not go about saying this work is superior to that. Working for society means giving up all thought of fame or profit and doing your duties. Pray single-mindedly to God for devotion and for the sense to serve with a pure heart."

*　　*　　*　　*　　*

"Service to the country may be rendered in many ways. Though serving society is good, it should not be begun with a craving for fame. The desire for fame will pervert the efforts of social workers in times of crisis. If a desire for fame or any other selfish attachment is patent or concealed in the heart, even the most noble efforts will be rendered futile.

" Don't we hear many patriots complaining, ' I strove so much for others and I have got nothing '? What is the cause of this regret and bitterness of mind? It is the result of working with a motive and not seeing it accomplished. If one starts serving his country or his society to earn fame and name, he will come to grief. This unholy desire will spoil any kind of good work. Whatever good we may do to benefit another or to serve society, we must dedicate it to God and resign ourselves to His grace. If we do so, we shall not be elated by success or depressed by failure.

" It will not be true service if we engage in work with the purpose of benefiting ourselves and with the desire for fame in our minds. It will be a kind of ' business '. It is true that great patriots who served their country have obtained fame and name. But such famous men did not seek fame. The secret of their renown and victory lies in their working without expectation of fame. And we have frequently seen that people who, forgetting this truth, began to work with the hope of similar renown, got sadly disappointed."

*   *   *   *   *

Some may ask how one can engage in social work without desire for fame or reward. If such doubters confine themselves to their domestic duties and lead lives of rectitude, they will have served society well enough that way. They need not enter the field of social service and feel regret or vexation.

It is difficult to do social service without attachment and desire. That is why Sri Ramakrishna
said, " Before you engage yourselves in social service,
obtain God's grace. First pray to God: ' Lord!
Fill my heart with devotion'."

To those who get lost in social work, this warning
of Sri Ramakrishna is very important. Many are
filled with regret that all the labour that they did
and all the money that they spent have been in vain.
The secret of this lies in the initial mistake in mental
attitude. That mistake has its effect like the drop
of buttermilk that falls into the milk pot and turns
it into curds. What else will be the fate of the edifice
reared on the foundation of the desire for fame and
name? It will surely tumble down and cause grief.
That is why Sri Ramakrishna Paramahamsa said:
" Before you enter on social service, pray to God.
Make your minds pure with the waters of devotion;
then begin to work. If the foundation is strong
and stable, then the building, howsoever raised, will
be secure."

What do surgeons do before they begin an opera-
tion? They wash their hands and knives with dis-
infectants and then begin to apply the knife.
Similarly, those who plan social work should first
make their minds clean. Then, by God's grace,
all will be well. There is no other means to success
in work and peace of mind. Muttering some
mantras will not suffice to produce the attitude of
utter surrender to God and the consciousness of
His supremacy. There is no use of mere dry ritual.

One must feel devotion in the heart. It is only after that one should begin social work of any kind. Work begun without invoking God's aid will be false and deceitful and will breed sorrow, anger and jealousy.

Not only should we, as Bhagavan Ramakrishna taught us, think of God and worship Him before we begin social work, but all the time that we engage in it, we must continue to work with the thought of God firmly implanted in our minds.

It is wrong to think that service to society and the worship of God are different things. All work must be done as worship of God. The thought of God will not be a hindrance to work. The practice of doing our work with devotion to God will give us great joy. It will give us skill and zest in our work. I can affirm without a doubt that this was the secret of Mahatma Gandhi's success. In everything that he did, in every plan that he made, in every step that he took he carried in his heart the thought of God which ever went with him as a man's shadow goes with him when he walks. This thought never hindered his work. On the contrary, it was the source of his success. In all the little tasks that we do, this thought of God will likewise stand by us like shadow and help us in silence. It is essential for a servant of society to labour with the thought of God unceasingly in one's mind. It is as indispensable to effective work as asepsis to surgery. A pure mind is a great asset and an unfailing *sadhana*. Devotion is the only way to get it.

5

XV. NON-DUALITY (ADVAITAM)

An Advaitin once asked Paramahamsa for his views on Advaita. The Advaitin said, " Brahman alone is real. The world we see around is false. This is the true Vedantic view, is it not? "

Bhagavan Ramakrishna said, " It is easy to argue and prove that the world around us is false, that it is all an illusion and the Supreme Brahman alone is the truth. But a logical proof of Brahman as the sole reality does not amount to experience or realization of Brahman. Between intellectual knowledge and spiritual experience, there is a world of difference. If we know that what is yonder is only a mirage, we will not seek to get a pot of water from it. If any one should ask us to go there for water we would ridicule him. If we know that what looked like water was only an illusion, we would act accordingly. What we do about a mirage depends on whether we know it to be a mirage.

" But this is not the case in respect of the truth of Advaita. By dialectics we reach the conclusion that the Supreme Brahman alone is true, that the jivas and the multiform things of the universe around us are only an appearance. Yet, the conclusion does not enter and transform our heart and mind. The conclusion that we have reached intellectually stands apart and does not touch and mould our life. It is not yet part of our inmost being. The conclusion that we arrive at by much learning and by much verbal argument remains with us like the burden on the donkey's back. It does not enter into our being. The professed adherents of the Maya theory, curiously enough, seem very anxious about their daily food and raiment. Trifles worry us and we lose our temper far too easily. Our knowledge of the truth does not always influence our conduct. Advaita is not an easy thing. It involves discipline and worship. We tremble with fear at the sight of a snake or a tiger. Knowledge obtained through the senses makes the entire body quake. When a hungry man sees delicious food, his mouth waters. The presence of food works upon one's body and life.

" When we meet a friend or a dear kinsman, we do not stop with merely identifying him. We feel a real joy, an inward thrill of delight. It is no use to affirm the validity of Advaita merely through logic. That will be like looking unmoved at the picture of a snake or a tiger.

" If a person truly attains the Advaitic wisdom, should he not, that very moment, feel at one with Supreme Truth? Even as the man trembles at the sight of a real tiger in the forest, he who has attained the true Advaitic wisdom should, that very instant, feel an abundance of bliss and become one with Brahman in a state of *samadhi*.

" If a man perceives the truth that Brahman alone is true and that all the rest is illusion, what room is there for the sense of difference? If the sense of difference does not vanish, the knowledge of this truth is indeed faint. It is not realized knowledge."

If Advaita is truly realized, the illusion of the sense of difference must vanish leaving no trace behind, like camphor that has burnt out. There will not be even the residual ash to proclaim, " I have burnt myself out." One who has attained the state of bliss knows the illusion as illusion and the truth as truth. But in that state there is no room for distinctions of " you ", " that ", " this ", "knowledge", "ignorance", " truth ", " negation ", etc. His life becomes one with the shoreless sea of silence. The being of one who has acquired the wisdom of Advaita merges in the flood of Brahman even as a doll made of salt dissolves away in water. Can the dissolved salt speak about the solution? When any one speaks in terms of " I know " or " I do not know ", the talk is with the consciousness of the differences of " I " and " you ". So long as his ego persists, how can the world become an illusion to him? When the sense of difference vanishes, there will be no room for further argument. All is silence.

This is the basic difficulty in Advaita, the difficulty of trying to elucidate on the plane of illusion a truth which mere intellect cannot grasp. The sense of difference indicated by " You " and " I " remains with the teacher who teaches and with the pupil who listens. To both of them, the world seems real in very truth. It is only in the state of *samadhi* that one can understand Advaita through actual realization. In any other state, all talk of Advaita is like an inflated bag. One can however swim, somewhat, with it. If one worships God with this knowledge, one may realize the Truth.

XVI. INCARNATION IN IMAGES

Before beginning to build a house, workmen first erect a scaffolding. They stand on this and build the house. When the construction is over, the scaffolding is unnecessary and it is taken away. Likewise, temples and tanks are unnecessary for men of ripe wisdom. Those who cannot concentrate their mind and keep it from wandering about need temple worship and purificatory baths.

If clay is fashioned with devotion into a Linga, it becomes God Himself. God who is present everywhere will not be absent from that Linga.

*   *   *   *   *

A person once said: "This idol is mere clay. We may not look on it as God."

Why do you call it clay or stone or copper? Why do you not see it is a form of God Himself? When God is in everything and when everything is in God, will not this form be as useful as any other for worshipping God? The clay image is God, the copper image too is God. There is nothing which is not God. Even a drop of water is a form of Parasakti. The water that we drink is also Parasakti. That which goes in and quenches the thirst—that too is Parasakti. If we utter the name of Hari with a rosary of *tulasi* beads, every bead is Hari's form.

Parasakti resides in the cloud in the sky, in the thunderbolt and in the flash of lightning. When the cloud falls as rain on a mountain and flows down as a majestic river, Parasakti dwells in that river as well. The devotee goes to the river at dawn and dusk and prays to the water saying, " O Water, may your joy fill me with joy. May your strength make me strong. O Water, brighten my eyes and broaden my sight. Even as a mother feeds her dear child with eager love, O Water, may your sweetness sustain me. O Water, purifying everything, you dry up and disappear. Grant that I may have that virtue and that purity. This is my prayer to you." With these words the devotee sprinkles the water on his head, and taking some water in the hollow of his hand drinks it, saying, " O imperishable Supreme! I bow to you." That water is Parasakti.

*   *   *   *   *

If we really perceive that God is everywhere, why should we not worship a divine form to help concentration of mind? Is the omnipresent One absent from that form? Those who do not care for image worship are not compelled to worship any image. It is, however, foolish to find fault with those who do. God is omnipresent. Parasakti is immanent in everything. We may worship even a particle of the cooked rice that we eat. If we eat the food after worshipping it, Parasakti will bless us from within us.

*   *   *   *   *

The image that is worshipped is not a symbol merely. The God that is everywhere is actually present in it. Our ancients considered the image that is worshipped as an incarnation in the idol. It is permanent incarnation like Rama and Krishna, God became incarnate in the stone and in the fish, in the boar and in Dasaratha's son. Even so, He becomes incarnate in the idol in the temple of Srirangam and in other holy temples. He is incarnate in this form in response to our devotion. The Alwars, Nayanmars and Acharyas with all their Vedantic realization saw God face to face in those holy temples. And, seeing Him there, they concentrated their minds on Him, meditated on Him, sang His praise and danced with joy.

There is a story about Ramanuja. Some children were once playing in the street. They drew on the ground a picture of the Srirangam temple and marked in it the recumbent form of Ranganatha. This was seen by Ramanuja walking on his daily round of mendicancy. Forthwith he fell prone before the figure and was lost in meditation of God. It is folly to think that God does not exist in the idols we make and the pictures we paint.

Once we realize that Brahman is present both in living and in non-living things, there will be no difficulty in regarding the consecrated idol as a form of the Supreme. Those who think otherwise, isolate Brahman and locate It in some other world. Apparently they have little faith in God's omnipresence. One may worship Brahman by thinking

and meditation. But that is not possible for every-
body. If this seems easy, this is a mere delusion.
But the worship of the omnipresent in an inanimate
Linga is within the capacity of anyone.

Belittling this mode of worship is wrong. It is
well known that Bhagavan Ramakrishna, the
Acharyas Sankara, Ramanuja and Madhwa and
many Christian seers and saints adopted the worship
of the incarnation in the icon and attained true peace
and bliss. So, we too may adopt an inanimate object
like a stone or a tree for our worship, meditate on
God and gain much good.

XVII. BHAJA GOVINDAM

" Sleep, my child, sleep, " says the mother. " I
am asleep, mother, " says the baby. This the child
says out of its love for its mother. It does not know
what is meant by sleep. One with mere book
learning speaks like this child. Without attaining
the state of samadhi, he says, " Sivoham, Sivoham "
(" I am Siva, I am Siva "). If the child really
sleeps, how can it say " I am asleep "?

When a man is in the grip of the ego, however-
much he may deny it, the qualityless Brahman
cannot help him. The only proper way is to practise
devotion thinking of Brahman as God and the whole
universe as part of His divine play. If that is done,
the self will ripen and in the fullness of time, it will
fall off from its stalk. To imagine that one is a *jnani*
when one is not, is of no avail.

Paramahamsa speaks thus humbly of himself before an Advaitic scholar:

" So long as the thought of my ego is troubling me with the consciousness of I, my Brahman will be only a qualified Brahman (Saguna Brahman). What harm is there in meditating on God and worshipping Him? I worship the Devi. She stands before me as the manifold *jivas* and objects of this universe. Bhagavati and Isvara are one. Is the diamond different from its lustre or the sun from its rays? You cannot see the one without seeing the other. The Devi whom I worship is the Brahman, the one without a second.

" It is no use merely muttering ' I am Siva ', ' Sivoham '; that consciousness can arise only when the ego is completely rooted out by devotion. Till then, ' I am God ' is not true. The truth is ' I am God's (slave) ' ' I am the instrument of His will'."

*   *   *   *   *

Once a sadhu was discoursing at length on Advaita at a place of pilgrimage. Ramakrishna who was there then had heard something dis-creditable to him. He went to the sadhu and said, " You expound the Vedanta wonderfully well! But people whisper something; what is the truth about it? "

" Oh, what of that? Why need a Vedantin bother if shadow sports with shadow? The whole world is an illusion. When the entire universe is false, will the lustful actions of my body alone be true? It is all a mirage. Why should you, a man of vedantic wisdom, worry yourself about it?" When Sri Ramakrishna heard this, he was filled with disgust, and he said: " Cast your Vedanta into the fire. Your scholarship is a big snare. You pamper your flesh by cheating foolish folk." It is dangerous for one without devotion to talk of the world as an illusion.

*   *   *   *   *

Duryodhana too once said, " God lives in me. It is He that prompts me to act as I do. I am not responsible. Why do you blame me?"

If a person really becomes God's servant and if he believes that all that he does is God's will, how can he do evil? The thought of evil will not taint him at all. Will a well-trained dancer ever make a false step? Without a thought and of their own accord her legs keep time. If the pure thought "I am God's man, everything is His dispensation" gets firm hold of one's heart, no impurity will approach it. Forgetting this, some learned fools quote scripture for their nefarious ends. They declare, " The whole world is an illusion and there is no harm in tasting the pleasures of the senses." They only deceive themselves. It is better to give up talk of this kind of Advaita and to engage in the easier path of devotion.

Even Sri Sankara Bhagavatpadacharya, that master of the Vedantic wisdom of the Upanishads and the Brahma-Sutras, addressed his marvellous intellect, and sang, " Foolish Mind! praise Govinda, pray to Govinda." When the great Sankara says this, where are we?

XVIII. SOCIAL REFORM

Many great reformers of our country have from time to time, effected changes in our modes of worship and ways of life. As a result of their teachings, however, only new traditions and new caste divisions have sprung up. This has led to men getting not reformed, but divided into new social groups. Reforms, inspired by the best of intentions, have unfortunately been the cause of division, of egotism, of mutual recrimination and disharmony. Our social differences have been the most enduring result of our social reform efforts!

The teachings and activities of Bhagavan Rama-krishna are singularly free from this defect. He does not find fault with any form of worship or any social practice. He saw the same Brahman every-where and he saw good in everything. Men became better by his teachings. No new practice arose in our land on account of him.

Though he was a great *jnani*, Bhagavan Rama-krishna did not speak against idol worship. He was a great Advaitin who had realized the Absolute in *samadhi*, and yet he did not despise apparently lower forms of worship. He viewed with equal respect every mode of worship of every deity. And his words accorded well with this wide vision.

Speaking once of the co-existence in Hinduism of the highest wisdom and various forms of rites and festivals, incantations and ceremonials, he observed: " The chief thing in paddy is the grain of rice inside it. We remove the husk covering the grain and then cook the rice. But then, my son, rice will not keep long. It will become rotten. If it is retained as paddy, it will last longer. And only the paddy will sprout if it is sown in the soil. True, it is the rice that sprouts, but it must get imbedded as paddy in the ground with the covering of the husk. It is to preserve our *dharma* and to give it the vital force to take root and grow that rites and ceremonies and festivals are prescribed. Rites are like the husk which covers the rice. We remove the husk when we want to eat the rice. To the man of wisdom, rites, festivals and temples, are unnecessary. But if *jnanamarga* alone were preached as the Hindu way to God and these rites were discarded, it would not take root and grow. It would die out and rot like the grain of rice sown in the soil.

" When you have a wound, you find that soon it is covered over. This covering protects it till it gets healed up inside. The covering must remain till the raw wound is healed. Then it dries up and falls off by itslf. When wisdom has been acquired, rites and rituals fall off and disappear of their own accord. To get rid of them before wisdom dawns, is like peeling off the skin before the wound heals and that will prevent its healing."

Some wise men think that one need not care for ceremonial rules. But it is not proper to dispense with them before wisdom matures. An artificially ripened fruit will not be as sweet as a fruit that has got ripe naturally after full growth.

The *jnanis* recognize no caste differences. This is a freedom that they acquire as a result of their wisdom. Sri Ramakrishna has a story to show how they use this freedom:

Once upon a time, Krishna Kishore went on a pilgrimage to Brindavan. Walking long had made him thirsty and he stood near a well. A man was drawing water in a pot from that well. Krishna Kishore implored him to give him water to drink. The man replied, " Sir, I am a pariah. You are a Brahman. It is not right that you should take water from my hands." " My man, " said Kishore, " can you utter Hari's name? " " Yes, I can, " replied the man. " Then, draw water uttering the name of Hari. It will be no sin if I drink that water, " said Kishore. The man drew some water uttering the name of Hari and Kishore quenched his thirst.

From this it is clear that Sri Ramakrishna taught social reform consistent with the ways of Jnana and Bhakti which are the bases of Hindu religion.

*   *   *   *   *

" In these days, men stress only important things. They do not like non-essentials. Therefore it is good to reduce rites and ceremonies." So taught

Paramahamsa in keeping with the spirit of the times.

To make *Kanji* properly, flour must be well mixed with some cold water and then it must be boiled. If hot water is poured on it even in the beginning, the flour will not dissolve properly; it will become lumpy. If one begins to reform society with too much heat and haste, conflicting social groups will arise like undissolved lumps of flour. Though one may see the urgent need for social reform, one must proceed cautiously and avoid the emergence of new groups and sects and thus ensure realization of the ultimate purpose of reform.

XIX. SELF-CONTROL

The wise teach the need for humility. Those who are learned in the Sastras practise humility as a means to realization. But far superior to this kind of humility is true humility of mind arising from regard for truth. Humility is not merely a means. In fact, of what avail are ourselves, our wealth, our intellect and our other possessions? Absolutely nothing. If we get rid of ignorance, the truth will make us humble.

When the son of a poor man, knowing he is poor, conducts himself accordingly, it is humility born of knowledge. To behave otherwise is folly. Even so, for any one, whatever his status or his riches, it is wise to walk humbly, knowing that riches and power will not endure. One must know the truth and be humble in truth. If, instead of that, one makes a parade of humility to earn the praise of others, it is not true humility.

A pupil went to his teacher and said: " I am the lowest of the low, I am a sinner. Show me the way (to save myself)." The teacher knew that the pupil had not yet seen the truth and that he talked the language of convention. Wishing to give him the light of knowledge, he told him: " Well, you go out and bring back something which is of less value than yourself."

" Oh! that is easy, " thought the pupil and went out. But when he went out into the world, he found that everything in the world was superior to him.

His heart ached to find that every other object, every living creature was purer and more useful to others than he. He was afraid that if he took any object to his teacher as of less value than himself, the teacher would think him proud. He did not know what he should do.

A thought occurred to him the following morning, as he sat down to empty his bowels. He thought: " My excrement is certainly inferior to myself. I shall take this to my teacher and tell him, ' This alone is inferior to me. Everything else is superior to me.' Surely, if I do this, my teacher would praise my humility."

And so, he took a broken tile and went to gather his excreta in it.

Suddenly a voice was heard, " You, sinner, do not come near me."

A vocie spoke from the filth and said: " What
you have done to me already is enough. Sinner
that you are, do not approach me again. Once I
was good food and sweet fruit. I was an offering fit
for God. The mouth of every one who saw me
watered with delight. To my misfortune, I came
within your reach, and you ate me. And this is
what I have come to, after I entered your body.
Once I was good to look at, good to eat. But now
men stop their noses at the very sight of me and shun
me. This is what you have done to me. Your
contact has brought me to this. Pray, do not come
near me again. For, if you do, who knows what
worse fate will befall me? Go awy from me."

Then the pupil understood how despicable he
was. He went to his teacher and said: " There is
nothing in the world inferior to me."

XX. WORTH ONLY AN ANNA
AND A HALF

It is possible to acquire thaumaturgic powers by
yogic practices. These " Siddhis " enable one to
perform miracles. They are wonderful powers
which seem to oppose natural laws. With the aid
of these powers, some yogis perform acts at which
others marvel. The disciples of these yogis go about
advertizing these " powers " and " miracles."

Bhagavan Sri Ramakrishna used to say that it
was improper to try to acquire such powers and to
make people wonder at them.

If anyone said, " In that town there is a yogi who has marvellous powers; come and see him ", Sri Ramakrishna used to reply: " Do not go there; do not go to see them, believing that you can benefit by seeing them."

Sri Ramakrishna did not say that the miracles which the yogis wrought were all bogus. He only taught that that was not the way to see God, that to acquire wonderful powers was not the proper way to worship God.

" These powers are thorny shrubs in the straight path of the seeker of Brahman. Do not get entangled in them. Do not get near those who claim to cure your ills by incantations, and to win your law-suits by yogic power. True devotees will not desire any-thing except God's grace. Certain powers may accrue by devotion, yogic practices and discipline. But they come of their own accord. True devotees will not seek consciously to acquire them.

" If we eat, we throw out faeces, urine and sweat. But nobody eats only to throw out excreta. True devotees will not practise devotion or yoga for the sake of attaining Siddhis. Siddhis are like the excreta."

By the acquisition of Siddhis, one's egotism increases. So, it is an obstacle to devotion and not a help to the attainment of God. That is why Sri Ramakrishna called Siddhi the " refuse " of yoga.

Here is a story which Sri Ramakrishna told: A yogi went to his teacher and said, " I performed penance alone in a forest for fourteen years and I

6

have acquired the power to walk on water." The teacher replied. " My son, why did you toil so hard? You have wasted fourteen years! For an anna and a half, the boatman will carry you across the water to the other shore. The Siddhi that you have acquired is worth only an anna and a half."

No one should waste his days seeking Siddhi. Practise true devotion to attain the grace of God. Do not join the company of yogis who wish to entice you by their miracles. That is Sri Ramakrishna's teaching.

XXI.   ROCK BOTTOM

Only a very small part of the universe comes within the range of knowledge. The mind of no man, however intelligent, can function beyond certain limits. What is truth? What is knowledge? What is the mind? These are un-solved riddles. So, all our researches are but riddles within riddles.

All things, animate and inanimate, sentient and insentient, are modifications of one primordial substance.

The bubbles that arise in water and the water itself are one substance. ' The bubbles arise in water, float and move on it and later disappear in the water with which they become one. Living beings are just like those bubbles. The water can be compared to the Supreme Being and the bubbles that appear on its surface to the several distinct *jivas*. God is the supreme Truth which includes and transcends everything. It alone is the vital force which appears in all living things. All of them ultimately are absorbed in It and disappear.

God is the sole reality. Living beings and lifeless things are like the bubbles that float on water. They cannot exist by themselves.

The Supreme Truth is like the Cauvery in floods. Our egotism creates the illusion that a handful of that water is the Cauvery itself.

The Vedantic quest may be compared to the act of a salt doll plunging into the sea to sound its depths. The moment it dives into the water, the salt doll is dissolved. What research can it do then? The *jiva* that seeks to measure God becomes one with God the moment it plunges into God. How then can it measure God's depths?

Man's body is like a pot. His brain and senses are like the rice, pulses and water which boil in the pot. The pot boils on the hearth. It will be hot if you touch the pot. If you touch the boiling rice, your fingers will be scalded. The heat in the pot and in the rice does not, in reality, belong to the pot or to the rice. The heat of the burning hearth becomes the heat in these things. Even so, Brahman transformed itself into the distinguishing qualities in living beings and lifeless objects. The activity of the brain and of the senses is in reality the work of Brahman. Not a grain of sand will move without Its power.

We ultimately come upon God whatever object we try to explore. In Salem District, wherever you sink a well, after a certain depth you hit rock. Brahman is like that. Whatever the object, however tiny or big, at its bottom there is this ground of rock, Brahman.

XXII.   CALL AND HE WILL COME

" What is the means to escape from Maya? " was a pupil's question to Sri Ramakrishna.

" God will show the way if there is a real desire to escape. To desire it is not merely to utter it in words. One should overflow with that thought and pant for it with all one's heart. With tears in our eyes, we yearn for wife and wealth. But who yearns for God like this?

" So long as the child is happy playing with its toys, the mother is busy working in the kitchen. Tired of its play and throwing away its dolls, the child begins to cry aloud. At once the mother leaves her work and runs to her child. In her hurry she might upset and scatter the things in the kitchen. In the same way, the Divine Mother will run to the side of the true devotee who cries out with a longing heart.

" In this Kali age, there is no need to do intense penance. It is enough if you meditate for three days with earnestness and fervour. Devi will dower Her children with Her grace. Be assured; this is no falsehood. My son, to attain Her, try and weep for Her intensely and truly for three days. You will succeed. Pray to Her with heart and voice for three days and say in truth, ' Divine One! Give me devotion, cast away my doubts. See that I never forget you. Cleanse me of my sins.' You will surely reap the benefit of such devotion. Earnest prayer will never be fruitless. Why doubt it? Look at me and be filled with confidence! " So spake Ramakrishna.

The child says, " Mother, wake me up when I become hungry." " It will get up of its own accord when it becomes hungry, " says the mother to herself. When God hunger springs up in you, no one need wake you up. And nobody need show you the way. We see this in the folk drama of the streets. At first by beat of drums and in loud voice people sing out calling for Krishna. But the man who acts the part of Krishna sits behind the curtain quite unconcerned, eating and talking. Then all the noise is stilled. Narada takes up his *Vina* and in low music sings, " Come, my Krishna ". At once Krishna bounces forward and stands on the stage.

Mere show and noise avail nothing. God has great love only for His true devotee. This incident in our street plays brings out this truth clearly so as to be understood by the simplest folk.

" Oh God! My Lord! " such words uttered by the lips have no effect. When the heart is full, the lips are sealed. Devi will listen to the cry from the heart of Her true lover. She will hasten to his side and bless him.

XXIII. THE CARPENTER'S WIFE

One of Sri Ramakrishna's disciples once obtained a government job, and put to him the question if it was right to work for wages. Sri Ramakrishna said. " My man, you took up the job to support your mother. What you did was right. It would have been wrong if there was not this need. Keep the appointment and serve God."

Some obtain wealth and power and become thereby proud and arrogant. Men think highly of the rich and powerful. But how long will wealth and power last? When we die, our wealth and power will not come with us. Why then should we make much of them? A rich man tends to forget that there are much richer men than he, compared to whom he is but a beggar.

As soon as it is dark, fire-flies rise in the sky. These flies, no doubt, think, " It is we who brighten up the whole world with our light. There is none like us." But very soon the stars begin to shine in the sky. Then the fire-flies become humble and ashamed. They realize, " Oh, those stars in the sky are brighter than we are. So, we must not think too much of our glory." Then the full moon rises and the stars become dim before her brightness. The moon shines in all its glory and thinks in its pride, " There is none so bright as I. I fill the whole earth with my light." Suddenly the eastern sky is bright with the sun. Where is the moon now? Look at this, be rich, and be modest, " said Sri Ramakrishna.

" Water flows freely under a bridge; it does not stagnate and emit a foul smell. Keep money moving in the same manner. Let it not stagnate in your hands. It may get impure and emit a bad odour. Allow it to flow and do good. Make money your servant. Take care that it does not become your master.

" Look at the carpenter's wife. With one hand she pushes the grain into the mortar. Her other hand pats the child on her lap. And all the while she is talking and higgling with the man who comes to purchase beaten rice. Though engaged in many things, she takes care that her fingers do not get crushed under the pestle. In the same way, though engaged actively in worldly life, keep God constantly in your mind and walk on the straight path.

" Look at that little lad whirling round and round that post. He clings firmly to the post. However fast he may turn, he keeps firm hold of the post. Even so hold fast to God and whirl round in worldly life.

" Look at village girls carrying water-pots on their heads. First a big pot on the head, on it a smaller pot, and on that a still smaller pot. Though all the pots are full of water, not a drop falls out as she walks. She walks along and talks about her family affairs and all kinds of things. You should lead your family life with the same skill. You should follow the straight path, unswervingly, whatever you do."

No harm will arise if everything is done in a spirit

of dedication to God. This is Karma-yoga and this is also Bhakti-yoga.

" When we cut a jack fruit, we smear our palms and fingers with oil. Then the jack gum will not stick to the hand. We can cut the jack and pull out the pulp. In the same way, we must lead our family life with steadfast devotion to God. If we do so, the attachments of wealth and pleasure will not stick to us. The mind too will not grieve in the face of trouble."

XXIV. RUMINATING

The milk of the cow permeates her whole body and is mixed with her blood. But can we get milk if we press her ears? No. It is from the cow's udder that we get milk. It is true that the whole world is filled with God. But its holy places are like the cow's udder. Devotees go there, receive into their hearts the devotion that swells up there like a fountain and reach God. God easily gives *darshan* in those holy places where many devotees for countless generations have performed penance and meditation. Here are deposited the penance, chanting, meditation, worship and prayer of innumerable devotees. And it overpowers the consciousness of the people who go there with piety in their hearts. This is what is meant by saying that it is enough if even a speck of dust from a devotee's feet touches us. The spots where countless devotees, learned and simple, have stood and worshipped have a sanctity all their own. Even stony hearts will melt in these places which have been hallowed by the song and dance of devotees. If we also, with hearts filled with devotion, bow down humbly there, we shall see manifest there the God who is invisibly present everywhere.

We may dig in the earth anywhere and obtain water. But in some places, there are wells, tanks and lakes already. We can go to them and easily quench our thirst. Similarily, our temples, holy places and holy rivers serve to quench our thirst of devotion.

*   *   *   *   *

We should make good use of these sacred places. Cows graze on the pasture to their hearts' content and then leisurely chew the cud in some shady spot. Even so we must go to holy places and perform worship, and then we must ruminate on our thoughts and feelings at those holy places.

We should not think our duty ended with the performance of a pilgrimage. We should not let go our devotion and pure thoughts. Sitting in a secluded spot, fixing the mind in meditation, we must seek to strengthen the devotion that filled our minds at the holy places. Else, we shall not benefit at all from the pilgrimage.

*   *   *   *   *

Merely going to a holy place or living there will not benefit us. It is content of mind that is important. Unless there is devotion in the heart, we cannot derive benefit from a holy spot. It is only if there is devotion in the heart that we can increase it by visiting holy places. If we do not have some devotion to start with, it is no use going to any holy spot.

Quarrelling with his parents at home, a boy may run away to Banaras or some other holy place. Taking up an appointment there, he may earn money and send some of it to his parents. But this is different from visiting Banaras for the sake or devotion.

Sri Ramakrishna once humorously remarked, " Mathuranath and I went to a holy place west of Calcutta. There mango trees and bamboo shrubs were very much like those we found in our own places. There was no difference. But one thing was noticeable. The people living in that holy spot had good powers of digestion. They seemed to digest everything they ate." What he meant to convey was that it was no good staying in a holy place and eating well, while having no devotion.

XXV. THE WAY TO BE SAVED

There are some people who say, " Look at King Janaka—a great King who was also a *jnani*. It is not impossible to be a *jnani* like him, while still living in the world." But they forget that there has been only one Janaka in history. To be a *jnani* doing one's duties, without attachment, in the world, one should practise silent, solitary meditation for some time at least. One should go through this discipline for a year, six months, or a month or at least for twelve days. During that period, one should ceaselessly think on God and pray to Him for His grace. Nothing in the world is to be regarded as yours or mine. This thought must take deep root in the mind. You must firmly realize that whatever you consider as yours will surely perish and disappear one day or another. One thing alone will surely endure. That is God. He is the one imperishable thing in us. God is the support of everything. He is all. With the one thought of attaining God, one should meditate with the sole desire and anxiety to attain Him. Do not mix with those who ridicule or despise meditation and devotion. Give up the company of those who treat devotees with disrespect or derision.

*　　*　　*　　*　　*

When your heart is unsteady pray to the Divine Mother of the universe. She will protect you. She will save you from the sins hidden in your heart. Tell yourself constantly that Iswari is beside you. If you do so, you will shrink with shame from evil thoughts and evil deeds. One who has received grace through meditation walks on the straight path untroubled in mind whatever his station and whatever may happen to him. He does his duties with humility and skill. We can see in him devotion to God, kindness to fellowmen, and rectitude in action. He is wise among the learned. He can also argue well like others. He behaves towards his parents with love and respect and without any flaw. He is loving to his friends and relatives. He is sweet of speech and helpful to others, and will earn the love and esteem of everyone. To his wife, he will be love personified. Only he who is thus disciplined should be called a *jnani*, though he may live with his family and apparently in the world.

The teachings of Bhagavan Sri Ramakrishna are not impractical ideas. They are truths which he verified in his experience and which he passed on to be adopted by others.

When he said, "The Devi stands by you; fall at Her feet; you will get whatever you want; She will save you from sins," he spoke from his own experience. If we realize that and act accordingly, we shall be saved; and our country too will prosper.

XXVI. YOUR OWN MOTHER

When people write their autobiographies, they select and record facts reflecting credit on themselves. They either suppress or disguise what is not creditable in their lives. A truthful autobiography will record many evil things which we thought of doing and from which we were saved by the grace of God.

We escape from sins by God's infinite mercy.

Were it not for His mercy, the fate of many great
and famous men would have been far differet.

But while it is true that we can be saved only
with His grace, we must not fail in our own effort.
Grace is like the wind. It is always blowing over
the sea. But the boatman must spread out his
sails to catch the wind; else the boat will not move.
We must spread out the sails of our hearts and profit
by the wind of God's grace.

*   *   *   *   *

There is no difference of high and low among the
duties that we should perform in the world. All
work is of equal value. Anything that we do should
be performed with devotion and the thought of
God implanted in our minds. Then, His grace will
fill our sails and push us onward. We shall obtain
by His grace the means and aids we need for our
tasks.

" A lamp lit in a house dispels the darkness of
ages. Similarly, if the lamp of God's grace is lit,
the accumulated sins of many lives will be destroyed
and the light of devotion will begin to shine."

" Holy one, people say you have seen God; help
us also to see Him." Thus said certain worldly men
to Sri Ramakrishna one day.

" If God so wills it, you too will have His *darshan*.
But you must also put in some effort. Do you desire
I should milk the cow, make the milk into curds,
churn the butter and spoonfeed you with it? "
said Bhagavan smiling.

When the breeze blows, we do not use a fan. We use it only when there is no breeze. If God's grace is on us, we may stop our effort. Then neither prayer nor meditation is needed. His grace alone is enough. But if the breeze of His grace does not blow, we shall need the fan of our effort.

As long as there is a sense of "I" and "Mine", His grace does not flow freely. If you think highly of yourself, He stands at a distance. When you give up your arrogance, then you set your sail to receive His grace and it will come to you abundantly. Our arrogance impedes the flow of His grace.

*   *   *   *   *

The child rolls in the dirt and heaps dust on its head. That is its nature. But the mother takes delight in washing the baby and making it tidy and enjoying its freshness. To err is natural for men; yet Iswari cleanses men of their sins. We are Her children. There is no need to fear. Love the Mother as your own mother. All your sins will disappear.

My son, do not seek to deceive the Mother. Adore Her. Iswari is the real mother. Indeed it was She who created you and everything else. Love Her as you love your own mother of whom you were born. And you will soon feel the good effect. Your body and mind will shine with lustre. You will have the same joy that a little child has when it lies on its mother's lap and smiles at her loving face.

XXVII. THE DEVOTEE

Even if a flint lies in water a thousand years, the fire in it will not go out. The moment you strike it with steel, it will emit a spark. In spite of years of immersion in water, its native fire remains and is waiting to come out. The devotion of a true devotee is like flint. It will be unsullied by contact with the world. It will remain steadfast in spite of every trouble and difficulty. His love of God is undying like fire in a flint. Even as the spark comes out when steel strikes the flint, the fire of true devotion will blaze forth when he hears God's name.

Trouble and ill report may assail the devotee. These are only trials of his faith. His devotion will survive them all and emerge, like gold, all the purer for being purged of dross.

Can one escape the delusions of sense-enjoyment? Yes, if one is fixed in the habit of blissful contemplation of God. When the higher bliss is enjoyed, the lower pleasures will lose their power. One who has tasted the bliss of the divine will not lose himself in the search for momentary pleasures which quickly turn into pain. Realizing that they merely distract the mind and do not give true joy, one would not willingly bring pain on oneself. One who has tasted sugarcandy will not care for a ball of dust and dirt. Will any one who has slumbered in a royal couch, lie on the bare floor of a dirty hut? The God-intoxicated man will not seek the pleasures of the body.

Whenever anything stirs up in you thoughts of
sensuous pleasure, instantly turn your mind to
God. If you practise this, you can overcome all
dangers. Remember that Iswari ever stands beside
you. In solitude, when no man sees you, She stands
near you. What danger can befall a devotee who
realizes this? All the wealth and all the beauty in
the world cannot tempt one who feels the Devi's
abiding and gracious presence by his side. True
devotion or worship does not care for fame. It is
marked by silence and solitude. Showy and noisy
worship is all futile pomp.

The waterfall shoots down the hill and gambols
on the rock and then swells into a majestic river.
Such is true devotion. It steps athwart all the
hindrances, doubt and delusions of life. It becomes
ever steadier and stronger. The devotee easily gets
over the griefs and confusions of the moment and
soon acquires equanimity of mind. The distur-
bances in a devotee's mind are but momentary.
They quickly subside in the bliss of devotion.

*   *   *   *   *

The devotee is the Lord's child. The tears that
he sheds are his strength. The signs of a Bhakta
are that his hair stands on end and tears flow down
his cheeks when he hears but one of God's names.
When these signs appear in you, you may know that
this is your last birth and that salvation is nigh.

XXVIII. WHY STILL FALSEHOOD AND DISHONESTY?

Our country has attained freedom. We have a republican form of Government. Our country holds an honourable place among nations. Our leader is praised and respected by the great men of the world. In spite of all this, why do we still behave like beggars and cheats?

Why do we believe that falsehood and dishonesty are ways to prosperity? Why do we act like mean people who live on garbage? Without realizing the greatness of Bharata Mata, why do we so basely degrade ourselves?

To the patriots who thus grieve and wonder, we may cite a story told by Sri Ramakrishna:

One day, a tigress attacked a herd of sheep grazing in a forest. The tigress, which was with child, gave birth to a cub as a result of the shock of its own assault and died on the spot. The cub lived and grew among the sheep. It grazed and bleated along with the young sheep, ignorant of its real nature. The tiger cub developed the qualities of a sheep.

A few years passed. Another tiger attacked the herd. The sheep were scattered and ran about. The tiger cub too started running away with the sheep. The attacking tiger saw the cub and wondered how it came to be there. He pursued it and with his jaws caught hold of its neck. The tiger cub bleated like a lamb. The old tiger took

7

the cub to a pond and showed it its reflection in
the water, and said "You, foolish child! You
and I belong to the same kind. Look, you appear
the same as I. Why do you run away like a sheep?"
So saying he threw to it a bit of mutton, and said,
"Eat it". At first the cub would not eat it. It
cried, "Ba, Ba", and felt an aversion to it. But
very soon it felt the taste of mutton. The tiger in
it began to assert itself. It ate up the whole piece
and asked for more. The tiger-nature, which was
all along dormant, now surged up with great force.

"Now, you know who you are, don't you? Come
along with me. You have nothing to do with the
sheep in the herd," said the big tiger.

Let us spurn and leave behind the qualities
belonging to our old bondage and let us quickly
assert our real, honourable nature. Poverty is
nothing to be ashamed of; but littleness of heart and
mind is. We may live honourably in poverty.
Let us not be bad men. May we cherish the new-
won glory of our motherland. Let us discard the
mean, cowardly qualities of falsehood and dishonesty.

XXIX. PRAYER

We must not be constantly petitioning to God
asking Him to do this thing and that thing for us.
We must instead just say, "Thy will be done,"
and be content to do His bidding. All holy
scriptures stress the need for this spirit of utter

surrender to God's will. But man's unregenerate
nature does not acquiesce easily. From time
immemorial we have been petitioners seeking
favours. With our lips we utter, " Everything is
Your grace, Your own," but in our hearts we crave
for this and that and expect God to grant us the
boons we seek.

God's decrees are not easy to understand. We
cannot truly know which is good and which is evil.
We do well, therefore, to leave everything to His
wisdom. This is the only correct course for us.
But there is no harm in sentient beings speaking to
God as they would speak to one another. That is
but natural. What harm is there in our speaking
out to God what is in our hearts? None at all.
Though God is the lord of all things, there is no
harm in speaking to Him in the form of prayer as
freely as a man and his wife speak to each other.
If we open out our hearts to Him without reserve,
sport with Him and talk to Him at least once daily,
our thought, speech and act will get purer. There
is no doubt that our hearts will be cleaned of their
dross. This is a truth which everyone can realize
by experience.

" How should we pray? Should our prayers
be silent and mental prayers? Are loud outpourings
of our feelings proper in prayer?" Sri Ramakrishna's teaching on this matter is this:

" We may do what pleases us best. Even if we
speak in a low voice, God will hear us. He can
hear the slightest movements even of small ants."

" Is prayer of any use? "

" When our hearts and tongues are in accord, our prayers will certainly have effect. But if one says aloud, ' All this is Thine ', but inwardly thinks ' It is all mine ' and prays to God, it will be useless. Do not seek to deceive God. You cannot fool him! Your heart and your act must be in unison. Pray with your whole heart and mind. God will grant your prayer. You are very dear to Him. Do your duty at the appointed time and leave the rest to God. Have no care! "

No danger will hit a ship so long as its compass is intact. Even as the needle of a mariner's compass always points to the Pole Star, if our mind is steadfastly fixed on God, we shall reach harbour safely enough!

It does not matter if you cannot offer worship to images in the way that other people do. But pray to Him saying, " I do not know whether You have form or not. I do not know what You are. I am ignorant. But, whatever Your nature, give me Your grace."

My son, none will take care of you so well as He. He will listen to all your prayers. He knows what is good for you. He will surely give you His *darshan* one day. He will appear before you at least when you are on the point of death. But do not give up praying to Him. In weal or woe, there is not another like Him with whom you can hold converse. Prayer is only holding converse with God. Men cannot remain dumb; they speak with others. Prayer comes under this law.

XXX. THE UNDYING LAMP

Men have become used to falsehood and dishonesty in the belief that these help them to get on. They brush aside morality, thinking that it is useless. But that is not the way of life. Dharma alone is good; it alone is happiness, skill and wealth. If dharma declines, a country cannot prosper. Everyone will become poor. Deceit and falsehood will ruin society. If society decays, all of us will be ruined.

Once a group of fisher-women were returning home late from a fair. They were delayed at the fair by rain. On their way home, they rested near a cottage close to a flower-garden. The gardener was a good man. " Spend the night here and go early in the morning, " said he. The fisher-women agreed and stayed.

The fisher-women could not get a wink of sleep in the night. They rolled on the ground but could not sleep.

There was a basket of jasmines in the room where they stayed. It was meant for sale the following morning. The fisher-women were overpowered by the fragrance of the flowers, and so they could not sleep. After a time, one of them stood up and said, " This ' foul smell ' does not stop but grows ever stronger. We must do something to put it down. " They took some water, sprinkled it on their fish-baskets and drew them near. The fish-odour overpowered the fragrance of the jasmines. The fisher-women slept soundly thereafter.

*   *   *   *   *

Everyone conceives of bliss after his own tastes. If good company and good habits do not govern us, bad ways will seem superior, and indeed essential to our life.

In this iron age there is only one penance which we need perform. That is to speak the truth. We say "No" even to that. Merchants, officers, all should speak truth. Truth alone is cleverness. That is the way to realize God as well as genuine success in life.

On some festive days we light a lamp that must not die out. It must always keep burning. If it goes out, we fear some mishap will befall the family. So also, the thought of God is an undying lamp set in our hearts. We should see that that lamp lit in our heart never goes out. Whatever we do, we must take care to feed the lamp with oil and trim the wick. Nothing will be hindered by it. True success will then be ours.

XXXI. KAMALA'S MIRROR

"Mother," said Kamala, "the mirror you gave me is useless. It does not clearly reflect my face."

The mother said, "No, Kamala. There is nothing wrong with the mirror. It is covered with dust now. You have to clean it. That is all." She then wiped the mirror with a piece of cloth and gave it to her child.

Kamala looked into the mirror and was delighted to see her face beautifully reflected in it.

This is the secret of seeing God in meditation.
If you keep your heart pure you will see God.   If
your heart is fouled by greed or lust, you will not see
God. Sri Ramakrishna was able to see the Devi
face to face because his heart was pure. And this
is the lesson of his life for us. Our hearts are like
mirrors. If they are pure and clean, they help us to
see God.

The trees and shrubs near a tank and the light of
the sky above it are all clearly reflected in its water.
But if a breeze stirs the water, the reflection vanishes.
It is the same with our vision of God. If there is no
dirt in our heart and no anger or hatred agitating it,
we can see the vision of God in our own hearts.   If
lust, anger and hatred dominate the heart, the vision
of God will fade away.

We must progressively accustom ourselves to
doing without many things.   We must firmly control
our desires for things big or small.   Commonsense
will help us here.   It will enable us to avoid useless
and vain talk and learn true detachment.

When we have brought our mind to this state,
God's form will be reflected in it as in clear, calm
water.   The world of desires and attachments is a
bottomless pit.   If a child peeps into a very deep
well, we would say to it, " Do not stand there; do
not peep into it.   Stand away from it."   Life is full
of unknown perils.   If we fall into them, we are lost
indeed.

Greed and anger are not easily got rid of.   If
we cannot quite get rid of them, we must turn them

in a direction where they will not be so mischievous. Lust after God. Turn your desires and power into the quest for God. Turn even your anger toward God! Show your impatience with Him for not giving you His *darshan*. When you feel anger against fellowmen, direct it towards God! So spoke the Paramahamsa. This is the way to purge and purify our nature.

* * * * *

We tame wild animals. We bring under control even an elephant and make it obey us. Our mind too can be tamed and controlled, if we make the effort. Do not let your mind wander uncontrolled in the wilderness. Worthless ideas abound like trees in a jungle. Allowed to feed on them, the mind will become a wild elephant. Then it will become uncontrollable. Wisdom is the goad with which we can bring the mind under control.

Attachments and desires should be steadily given up. If they are allowed to grow, wisdom will perish. An overgrowth of weeds will kill any plant. If the weeds are removed, the plant will flourish. An overgrowth of desires and attachments will choke the tender plant of wisdom.

XXXII. SAVING ONESELF AND
PREACHING TO OTHERS

Many persons seek to teach us our duties (*dharmas*) through religious discourses and the exposition of holy stories. These are of course very learned persons and their efforts spring from worthy motives. But if men are to be reformed, the force of true devotion should reinforce the preaching of religion. The preacher's own devotion should touch the listener's heart. Else, the most learned discourse will be useless.

Bhagavan Ramakrishna was once asked his opinion about religious preachers.

He replied: " The ordinary preacher is like a man who invites a hundred persons to a feast when he has barely enough to feed himself. His devotion can scarcely secure his own salvation. How then can he instil devotion in the hearts of others?

"We must first of all install God in our own hearts. We may then seek to teach others. We cannot preach renunciation and devotion to others when we have not ourselves got rid of lust and anger. It is easy to preach to others. But such preaching will be like ringing bells and blowing conches in a ruined temple where there is no consecrated image."

*   *   *   *   *

In spite of our own imperfections, we may indeed seek to guide others on the path if we surrender ourselves to God with absolute devotion.

Bhagavan Ramakrishna tells the story of his meeting with such a person. " Well, Sir, ' said Paramahamsa to him, " you preach the *dharma* with great vehemence. Your own life has not been very correct. Still you captivate other men and lead them to devotion. What is the secret of this? "

The man replied, " I am indeed the lowest of the low. But the grace of God can work wonders. You know a dirty broom is useful for cleaning the streets. I am such a broom in the hands of God. He uses me to sweep the dirt off the hearts of men."

Sri Ramakrishna felt he had no answer to this.

*   *   *   *   *

When there is true devotion in a person's heart, God Himself dwells in it and no blemish can stand in the way of his devotion going into the hearts of others, even as no cloud can stand in the way of the sun's rays spreading light and heat.

XXXIII.   HAVE NO DOUBT

" Do not be anxious as to how you can control and change your nature. Charcoal is jet black. When fire is applied to it, it glows; its original blackness disappears. Even so, in contact with the fire of knowledge the impurity in your heart will vanish."

Keep your heart pure and free from taint. Your power to do good will then be enormous.

White cloth fresh from the laundry will take on any colour you apply to it. Our mind is like a piece of cloth fresh from the laundry. Good company and honest effort will turn it in the direction of God. Listen to the speech of the English-educated. They use many English words. Sanskrit scholars use many Sanskrit words. The minds of those who keep good company can never be turned to evil. Those who keep bad company will be ever thinking about evil things. Men's thoughts will be dyed the colour of their company. Good company will promote virtuous thoughts. Evil company will promote vicious thoughts.

Let us not deceive ourselves. Truth and devotion are the only means to reach God. If we forget God, we shall die. Without devotion, we cannot truly live.

Jnana and Bhakti are not different. Devotion and Truth together make up Wisdom.

To kill others, you need a sword or a rifle. A needle will do for committing suicide. Likewise, one must know much for teaching others and dispelling their ignorance. To bring God into one's own heart one needs no great learning. Devotion will suffice.

Devotion is the root of all religions. If there is real devotion in a person, his religion will serve his needs. Without devotion one cannot attain wisdom through learning or through conversion to other religions.

*　　　*　　　*　　　*　　　*

" My cow will eat this and not that." So saying, a cowherd feeds his cow with things of his choice.

The cow barely smells them and turns its head away.
It does not yield much milk. But the cow that grabs
anything and eats it with gusto yields plenty of rich
milk.

The milk of wisdom cannot flow freely from a
mind given to doubting.

*   *   *   *   *

A man suffering from thirst will seek to quench
his thirst, somehow, even with muddy river water.
He will not start digging a well there in search of
pure water. Similar is the thirst for God. Those
who thirst after God will not go seeking new religious
beliefs because their own seems contaminated. Nor
will they seek to found a new religion for themselves. If one is truly thirsting for God, he will try
to quench his thirst with the aid of his own religion.
He will not waste his time devising new religious
beliefs.

A devotee's desire for God is like a miser's craving
for money. He will pant for God like a drowning
man gasping for breath.

Sri Ramakrishna said; " Some people speak
with scorn of blind faith. I cannot understand their
attitude. What do they mean by blind faith?
There is no special kind of faith called blind faith.
There is wisdom and there is faith. Faith has no
eyes. All faith is blind! "

*   *   *   *   *

If we seek to live a life without God, we shall
only meet with disaster. We must cast off all

doubts and develop deep devotion. The world has not sprung out of nothing. Can man's life and thought spring from the void? We need have no doubts about the existence of the Supreme or of the reality of God's grace.

Do not be bothered by thoughts of hell. Think of God and pray to Him and say, " I have done many forbidden things and I have omitted to do many things that I should have done. Take pity on me, O Lord! " All your sins will vanish. So says Bhagavan Ramakrishna Paramahamsa.

XXXIV. ADVICE TO A GRANNY

In a conversation with Keshab Chandra Sen, the Chief of the Brahmo Samaj, Sri Ramakrishna Paramahamsa once said, "What is the use of praying to God, saying: You created the universe. Your greatness is beyond words. You did this; You did that?

" Sitting before his father, does a son exclaim, ' Aha! My father has so many servants, so many horses and carriages, so many gardens.' ? No. A loving son does not thus reckon up his father's worldly estate. He does not think particularly of even his father's love. He takes it all for granted.

" We are God's children. His love is a law of nature. There is no need to affect wonder at it or even to speak, or think of it. We must not waste time in vain talk of all this. We must seek rather to reach God straight. We must approach Him as a wife approaches her husband or a child its mother. We may ask Him familiarly to do this or that for us even as a wife asks her husband or a child its father. You will not clasp Him to your bosom by keeping at a distance from Him. You must not be afraid of going near Him. Believe that God is your own and nearer to you than any kinsman of yours. You can deal with Him with absolute frankness and intimacy."

This is the secret of the way of devotion. In devotion, there is no fear or wonder or even humility. The marks of devotion are love, confidence and faith. In the beginning there may be hesitation and even fear. When devotion grows, they will give place to confidence. The devotee will then approach God with a feeling almost of proprietorship.

*   *   *   *   *

The mother of one of his disciples came once to Sri Ramakrishna and said, " I have become old. I wish to cast away the cares of family life. I wish to go to Brindavan and lead a life of renunciation in the presence of Radha."

Paramahamsa felt that this would not be really possible for the old woman, that her detachment was fancied and that she was not quite free yet from attachment to the family. So he said to her:

" Mother, I know your love for your grand-daughter. Wherever you go, to Brindavan or

elsewhere, you will carry with you the thought of
your grandchild.   You will be wondering if in your
absence she is being taken care of properly.   Your
body may be in Brindavan, but your thoughts will
be centred on your grandchild.   But try to look on
your grand-daugher as Devi and show your love to
her.   Remain in the family and take care of the
child, disciplining your mind to think of her as
Radha.   All your love for the child will end in devotion to Devi.   When you fondle the child, when you
feed it, when you put the mark on its forehead,
imagine that you are doing all this to Devi. Then
though you may be living in your own place, you
will get the benefit of renunciation and of the worship
of Krishna in Brindavan."

*   *   *   *   *

Sri Ramakrishna taught: " Whomsover you love,
whether it be a child, mother, father or friend, get
used to thinking of that person as Divine, as
the embodiment of Devi.   That is the easy and
unerring path for all of us.   That is the way to purify
our lives."

XXXV.   WHERE IS GOPALA?

Ramaswami Padayachi got up one midnight.
He went to the cottage of his friend Sengodan in
the neighbouring forest.   He knocked at his door,
calling him by his name.   Sengodan woke up and

said, " What do you want? Why do you wake me
at this hour? "

" I want a match to light my cheroot."

" How funny! " exclaimed Sengodan. " Why
did you not light your cheroot with the lamp in
your hand? "

Ramaswami had not realized that there was fire
in the lamp in his hand.

Sri Ramakrishna related this story to show the
folly of those who seek God somewhere outside
themselves, not knowing that all along He resides
in their own hearts.

Pointing to his breast, he said, " If a man sees God
here, he will see Him present in the whole world
outside.

" If a man does not see God in his heart, he cannot
see Him anywhere else. If he sees Him in the temple
of his heart, he will then be able to see Him in Kashi
and Kanchi. He will then realize that the whole
universe is a vast temple of God. So long as one
does not realize God in the heart, but seeks Him
afar in the regions of the sky or beyond, we may be
sure one is enveloped in ignorance. When
the lamp of wisdom is lit, God will shine in the
temple of one's heart.

Seeing God in one's heart does not consist in
merely accepting another's statement about it. One
must comprehend it with all its manifold implica-
tions and fashion one's life accordingly. The man
who has realized God in his own heart will lead a

truly transformed life. He will be like a man who
was looking for a long-lost purse and found it in his
own pocket. Imagine a mother dreaming that her
child is lost. She searches for him in her dream
and weeps over her lost child. Suddenly she wakes
up and finds her child sound asleep beside her.
How she will rejoice! Think of it. We shall feel
a similar joy on realizing that God is in our heart.

*   *   *   *   *

One day Yasoda asked Radha in great anxiety,
" Where is my Gopala? He has not yet returned
home. Do you know where he has gone? "
" Mother! Do not be anxious. Close your eyes
and meditate on Gopala. You will see him at once."
Yasoda did so and had a vision of her darling
Gopala.

Yasoda then sought a boon of Radha. She said
to her, " Radha darling, your power is the fruit of
your devotion. Will you not let me have it too?
Show me the way." Yasoda got the boon.

We too, all of us, like Radha and Yasoda can
see Gopala everywhere and always. But we must
yearn for Gopala as Radha and Yasoda did. The
longing must spring in the heart. As the Katho-
panishad says the vision of God will surely come to
us if we seek it with sincere longing.